KARL HF

THE MIDDLE AGES

Background Studies
on the
History of Western Culture

Translated by Johanna Collis

Steiner Schools Fellowship Publications

Translated from
Studienmaterialien zur Geschichte des Abendlandes,
Band II, Mittelalter,
Verlag Freies Geistesleben, Stuttgart 1985.
The translator also took account of the 1956 edition
which was published by Karl Heyer.

Edited by John Anderson

Front Cover: Designed by Brien Masters
incorporating the drawing by Brian Gold
of a sculpture at Erfurt Cathedral.
Text design by Jacqueline Niven.

ISBN 0 9510331 7 4
Copyright Steiner Schools Fellowship 1994

Printed and bound in Great Britain by Penwell Press

CONTENTS

DEDICATION

This production is dedicated to the memory of Jesse Darrell (1906 to 1991) whose life was devoted to Rudolf Steiner (Waldorf) education and to the source from which it springs: anthroposophy. His major contribution was as a class teacher (for some 40 years), a history teacher, a religion teacher and a holder of the school services. He lectured in more than one continent on a variety of subjects in teacher training courses and was consulted eagerly by a stream of colleagues right up until his death. He was past master at story-telling and his anecdotes were legion.

As history, and the development of human consciousness, were perhaps closest to his heart, this particular work of Karl Heyer's was chosen as something that would be an appropriate and worthy memorial to him. He often remarked how valuable an English translation would be. His own copy was amongst the most thumbed volumes in his extensive library.

Many of his friends - too numerous to name here - through their financial gifts, have contributed towards this production; their generosity is hereby gratefully acknowledged. But the work of three of them deserves special mention: Johanna Collis who undertook the considerable task of translating from German to English, John Anderson who has acted as editor and Brian Gold who has designed the artwork for the front cover, interpreting as part of it a magnificent yet enigmatic thirteenth Century sculpture at Erfurt. The gift of their expertise not only reflects the admiration, love and respect which so many friends had for Jesse Darrell, it is a tangible reminder for us of the inspiration and enthusiasm that so very many felt in their daily lives and for their life's tasks after conversations with him.

Finally, a word of thanks to Verlag Freies Geistesleben, the original publisher, for permission to publish the work in English.

Brien Masters
Steiner Schools Fellowship
Forest Row 1993

FOREWORD

The interest given to Francis Fukuyama's ideas on the 'end of history' shortly after the collapse of Communism in Eastern Europe is more indicative of our growing disorientation amidst the overwhelming information of global events than of any seriously considered new outlook on the historical process. While society has never been better informed, seldom has it been so poorly served by its political leaders and leading intellectuals in finding its bearings in a world manifesting pathological symptoms: the increase in group violence, the disenfranchizement of large numbers of people, the tacit approval of lying - 'being economical with the truth' - at the highest levels of government, a purely bureaucratic approach to contemporary problems and crises. Such symptoms as a whole have contributed to the steady increase since the mid-1950s in individual anxiety and depression.

Similar signs of disorientation can be found in geography. Not a few wry smiles were raised after testing had shown that only a small minority of secondary pupils in the United States could locate Europe on a global map. Similar studies discovered that English pupils were only marginally more astute when asked to locate particular European countries. Undoubtedly a new interest in geography teaching at the primary and secondary levels has begun outwardly to remedy this lack of knowledge, but the cause of the inner disorientation lying behind such facts will not have been addressed.

Human beings learned first to fix their physical position on the earth by referring to the starry heavens and planets. The 4,000-year journey in consciousness from Stonehenge to the use of the sextant and compass is not as great as that from these instruments to the use of satellites capable of quickly determining the position of any ship or location possessed of the necessary equipment. It could be metaphorically said that we must discover the inner equivalent of sextant and compass in order to find our bearings in the flow of historical events that threaten more and more to overwhelm us.

The modern materialistic science, of which history is often said to be a part, is not able to distinguish objective historical necessity from chance. What so frequently appears as historical analysis attempting to show the root causes of certain problematic events usually harks back to some earlier event or occurrence, itself simply a fixed point in a long series of happenstance.

If this seems an overly harsh judgement of modern-day historical studies, let it be remembered that the popular conception of history is more often today the determining factor. All too seldom do the insights of a leading historical thinker such as a Barbara Tuchmann catch the attention and imagination of the media.

The pallid concepts so often applied in trying to understand and interpret current events need to be transformed. More substantial concepts will only be possible when more people are willing to work on these concepts for themselves in the manner pointed out by Ralph Waldo Emerson over a century ago. The challenges and difficulties of the task are only too apparent as we reconsider the approaches taken by the West to the 1991 Iraqi invasion of Kuwait or the somewhat later disturbing events in former Yugoslavia.

Karl Heyer's stated purpose during the 1930s in presenting his historical insights as study material 'to learn to stand rightly within our own time in the light of a deepened understanding of the history that has brought us here' is all the more urgent when those in power respond to events out of an evermore superficial understanding of the forces moving behind them. The answers needed will only come through a much finer perception of what lies in the depths of the human soul: 'The increasing mechanization of the external world throws human beings back upon their own inner resources. Only in the depths of their own being can they find the principle of life that will one day work its way outwards again from within towards the world.'

Anthroposophy, a science of the spirit, is a modern path to these inner depths of the human soul where this principle of life is to be found. Rudolf Steiner, in speaking of the laws of necessity, pointed out that when attempting to understand how the past works in individuals we should first look to their inborn, characteristic gestures. With sufficient effort, and with insights anthroposophy is able to provide, such gestures give us a clue as to how a certain individual has thought in a former life on earth. If, similarly, we are to look for the true facts which could bring us eventually not only to a deeper understanding of historical events but out of this understanding to approaches and solutions to problems that the modern world situation demands, must we then not begin to find the gestures in history and current events as well?

The first North American newspaper appeared in Boston in 1690. It provided coverage of newsworthy events once a month, 'oftener,' the editor explained, 'if any glut of occurrences happen'. The glut of occurrences brought to our attention daily, and even at times hourly, has become a register of troubling events to which few, if any, effective solutions appear. The speed at which we are being asked to assimilate these events makes the very type of observation called for certainly very difficult. 'If what we observe in individual gesture is to be understood as the residue of past lives on earth, born with the individual into an incarnation, surely it is not complete nonsense to assume something like gestures in what we encounter in the facts of history?' asked Rudolf Steiner in a lecture a year after the outbreak of the first World War.

Karl Heyer (1888-1964), as a dedicated student of anthroposophy and history, set himself the task of working not only with these outer historical gestures, which can reveal the inner necessity, but also with their relationships to one another. The fruits of this work, encompassing the development of western civilization from pre-history up to the twentieth century, he published as study material in nine volumes. With a directness of style he leads the reader without delay into the kind of historical observation and interpretation which arises when the historian's efforts are focused on finding the gestures in the historical record which can reveal those forces of evolution moving the events themselves. By being shown, however succinctly, how these forces are transformed in the gestures found in events of later epochs, the reader is familiarized with a way of observation and thinking that orientates rather than disorientates. The view is directed away from what ultimately amounts to a register of events. What we are so in need of is just such a mode of observing and thinking about history which can actually reveal the necessity and meaning working behind events, which is so elusive to find. Herein lies Karl Heyer's contribution.

This is the first volume of Heyer's historical work to appear in English. It is hoped it will become more than helpful to teachers in Waldorf schools; to seminarists in anthroposophical training centres looking to deepen their understanding of the evolution of consciousness; and to those familiar with anthroposophy. It can also prove thought-provoking for general readers searching for new insights and willing to keep an open mind for concepts based upon the substantiality of soul and spirit.

John Anderson
Vindbyholt, Denmark,
1993

THE GERMANIC PEOPLES

In the spiritual science of Anthroposophy our modern age, the fifth post-Atlantean era, is sometimes called the Germanic or Anglo-Saxon era[1] to indicate that the Germanic element as such is the main bearer of its culture. The Latin peoples in this era secure the continuity of evolution by preserving the cultural heritage of Greco-Latin times. The Germanic peoples in the main carry forward the development of the consciousness soul; the Anglo-Saxon above all the outward-looking consciousness soul; and the central European primarily the ego, the core of the human being as it is manifested within the consciousness soul.

During the fourth post-Atlantean era the Germanic peoples underwent their childhood and youth. When they first appeared on the stage of world history more or less at the beginning of Christian times they had reached the phase of the sentient soul. They stood 'at a point in their development that may be described as a transition from a bodily astral consciousness to a consciousness befitting the sentient soul. Mankind as a whole had stepped across this threshold in the transition from the ancient Persian to the Egypto-Chaldean era.'[2] The Germanic peoples lived strongly in their mythology, and their experience of the world was founded on ancient powers of clairvoyance. They still enjoyed that state of 'historical grace' which allowed them to look into the spiritual world and bring down primeval perceptions, livingly experienced, into what had to be established in the physical world.[3] Then came the 'twilight of the gods' as the ancient clairvoyance faded, so that in the Middle Ages the Germanic peoples, filled with the cultural heritage of Antiquity under the guidance of the Church, made relatively rapid progress through the stage of the intellectual soul which had been developed to the highest perfection by the Greeks and Romans. Perhaps it would be more accurate to say that, while the masses remained much longer in the element of the sentient soul, those educated by the Church soon attained the stage of the intellectual soul. Finally, as the modern age of the fifth post-Atlantean era dawned, the impulse of the consciousness soul awoke powerfully in these people in whom it had been dormant hitherto. At this moment they began to unfold their true nature and assume the role of representatives and pioneers for mankind at large for this era.

Rudolf Steiner frequently pointed out that the Germanic peoples were still entirely immersed in the old consciousness of the group soul when they first appeared in history . 'If you were to go back to ancient peoples

1

and races you would find that originally human beings formed small groups. In the case of the Germanic peoples you would not even have to go back all that far. The writings of Tacitus give a strong sense of the way an individual member of one of these peoples felt his tribe to be more important than his own individuality. An individual member of the Cherusci or the Sigambri felt himself to be one with his tribe rather than a personality in his own right, and so every individual was responsible for the fate of the tribe as a whole. Therefore it didn't matter who carried out revenge for an insult aimed at another individual or at the tribe. As time went on individuals began to step outside the tribe, which was thus breached and no longer stood as a compact unit. In the same way human beings in general have evolved away from the group soul and gradually risen to an experience of the ego within the individual personality.'[4]

It has not always been the case 'that human beings could say "I" to themselves as they do today. In the days when the Cherusci, the Heruli and so on, occupied the territories now inhabited by the Germans, an individual felt himself to be a member of his tribe rather than an individual human ego. Just as fingers do not experience themselves as being separate from the hand, so did individual Cherusci not feel that they had to say "I" to themselves. The "I" was the ego of the whole tribe; the tribe was an organism, and groups of people related to one another by blood possessed a kind of common ego-soul.'[5]

Within the tribe, the next smaller blood-related group in which the individual was embedded was the clan, the extended family that in turn encompassed even smaller groups or families of close relatives. The strength and significance of these close-knit groups is also described in Tacitus' *Germania*.

Reporting on their battles, he says: 'It is a principle incentive to their courage that their squadrons and battalions are not formed by men fortuitously collected, but by the assemblage of families and clans. Their pledges also are near at hand; they have within hearing the yells of their women, and the cries of their children. These, too, are the most revered witnesses of each man's conduct, these his most liberal applauders. To their mothers and their wives they bring their wounds for relief, nor do these dread to count or to search out the gashes. The women also administer food and encouragement to those who are fighting.' (*Germania 7*)

Here is another passage that tellingly describes their sense of family and their relationships with one another: 'Children are regarded with equal affection by their maternal uncles as by their fathers: some even consider this as the more sacred bond of consanguinity, and prefer it in the requisition of hostages, as if it held the mind by a firmer tie, and the family by a more extensive obligation. A person's own children, however, are his heirs and successors; *and no wills are made.*[6] If there be no children, the next in order of inheritance are brothers, paternal and maternal uncles. The more numerous are a man's relations and kinsmen, the more comfortable is his old age! nor is it here any advantage to be childless. It is an indispensable duty to adopt the enmities of a father or relation, as well as their friendships.' (*Germania 20, 21*)[7]

In his lectures on Germanic, Norse mythology, Rudolf Steiner described the gradual ascent to the ego as it took place in Europe (as opposed to the Orient): 'The Germanic, Norse individual felt encumbered by a group soul . . . This was why even Tacitus was still able to describe the tribes of central Europe in the way he did . . . He saw how members of the tribe felt they belonged to the tribal ego. But gradually the individual ego was born out of the tribal ego, and people felt that the god Thor was the one who granted them their own individuality. At the same time they felt that this god was bound up with the overall spirit of their tribe and with all that lived in its group soul. This group soul was termed Sif, and Sif was the wife of Thor . . . Sif and Thor were felt to be the beings who granted the ego to the individual human being.'[8]

Thus is the birth of the ego presaged in Norse mythology. This birth is laid down in the very nature of the Germanic peoples from the beginning, which is not the case, for example, with the peoples of the Orient. An Oriental entered into the great universe at death, whereas a member of a Germanic tribe in Europe united with 'a single valkyre, a single higher soul; at the moment of death one's own valkyre was there. Everything is individual and personal.'[9]

The valkyre took up the warrior who had met his death on the battle field. Resolute courage, valour and personal capability were the characteristics most esteemed and most highly evolved in Europe,[10] and the Germanic peoples, more than any others, developed these qualities. In the Orient, on the other hand, the flowering of culture was not seen in resolute courage and valour but in the cultivation of ancient wisdom.

In earlier times, resolute courage and valour went hand in hand with an unruliness of soul. In Rudolf Steiner's description[11] the people of the Nibelungen age have an instinctive, elemental life of feeling; there is something wild and primeval about them. The landscape of Europe, too, was very different then; great tracts of land were bare or covered with forest. Only gradually did the landscape change as the forest was cleared and the land made arable with meadows and cornfields. In a certain sense Rudolf

Steiner saw the older, Nibelungen phase extending right up to around AD 1200, when the Nibelungen poetry came into being. With the rise of the European towns came a culture of citizenship that replaced the old unruliness of soul and relatively primitive nature of the people. Walther von der Vogelweide stood at the beginning of this, and it finally reached its culmination in Goethe. This was the one stream, the one that led on into the future. Beside it flowed another important and externally influential stream in which much of the old Nibelungen element with its characteristic attitudes of soul continued to flourish well beyond 1200: the central European princes and their followers. These two streams continued to flow side by side through the history of central Europe.

*

The characteristics of the sentient soul in its Germanic nuance reappear in Germanic law and its successor, the German law of the Middle Ages, up to the time when Roman law was 'received'. A considerable amount based on spiritual science has already been written about this Germanic-German law and the social structures connected with it, so in the main we need only direct the reader to these works[12] while providing a brief summary here.

In keeping with the social structures of the sentient soul stage, the dominant reality in the life and the law of the Germanic peoples was the clan, the extended family. Rudolf von Jhering said quite rightly: 'It is possible to make the general statement that the degree of external, legal organization of the family is the reverse of the degree of maturity of a state: the more imperfect the latter, the more structured the former, and vice versa . . .'[13] In early Germanic times and even in the Middle Ages there was no such thing as a 'state' in the sense of a rational structure, so we would do well to avoid this term in that context in order not to raise erroneous ideas. The clan uniting blood-related individuals was the soil on which the social and legal life of the Germanic peoples grew. Characteristically enough, the Gothic word *sibja* (German *Sippe* = clan) also means peace, an alliance, and one's relations.[14] The individual is embedded within the peace of the clan. If the individual or the clan is harmed, the whole clan wreaks revenge by entering into a blood-feud not only with the perpetrator but with the whole of his clan. Ludwig Thieben[15] described the way a blood-feud arises out of an experience of wrath, and wrath is characteristic of the sentient soul with its instinctual nature emerging out of the blood forces. Someone expelled from the clan is 'devoid of peace', indeed he is hardly human any longer since he

4

now bears the head of a wolf, *gerit caput lupinum.*[16] For ancient clairvoyant consciousness the wolf was the power that opposed the good, light, sunlike forces that had for centuries lived and worked in the blood and in the peaceful communities founded on consanguinity. The wolf Fenrir, for example, devours the sun; and it is not for nothing that a she-wolf is the symbol of Rome, for it was the task of Rome to wrench the individual human being out of the ancient, holy relationships founded on blood ties and make of him an individual.[17]

Another aspect of Germanic law is the way it is filled with elements that can only be understood on the basis of the ancient consciousness of instinctive clairvoyance. Rudolf Steiner pointed out[18] that old Germanic law gave a father the right to decide whether the newborn child laid at his feet should live or die. According to Steiner the child did not belong to the earth in a spiritual sense until it had taken earthly nourishment; it remained as much within the sun's sphere of influence as it did as an embryo inside the mother's body. This was still perceived clairvoyantly in ancient Europe. But once even the smallest drop of milk had been swallowed the father no longer had the right to destroy the child, for then it belonged to the earthly realm.

Another legal institution that is particularly foreign to modern consciousness is that of the ordeal (*iudicium dei*). This was practised in ancient societies including that of the Germanic peoples, who continued to use it well into the Middle Ages. It involved powers that still existed then but have since changed. Rudolf Steiner mentioned the ordeal by fire: 'In this ordeal the endeavour was to discover the guilt or innocence of a person by making him walk across a red-hot gridiron. If his flesh was burnt he was considered guilty, but if he crossed unscathed he was held to be innocent. People today view this as a superstition, and yet it is true. It involves a capacity people used to have which they have since lost. In earlier times an innocent person, filled - in a solemn moment - with the knowledge of his innocence, and knowing himself to be safe in the bosom of divine spirits because he was utterly convinced of his connection with the spiritual world, experienced his astral body being detached from his physical body. At that moment he could walk across the red-hot coals without harm. This is how it was in earlier times. It is perfectly true . . .'[19]

Let us look once more at the way the old groupings of the Germanic peoples metamorphosed. In his lectures on the Middle Ages Rudolf Steiner stated that at the time when Christianity was being founded the Germanic peoples as a whole had reached the stage equivalent to that described by

5

Homer for the ancient Greeks. The individual members of a tribe were bound together by ties of blood and the tribes knew about their descent from a single family. They were regular family groups, not hordes, and out of the individual families grew the relationship to the tribe. This was the stage of the Germanic peoples at the time of the great migrations.

'By the end of the fifth century a degree of stability and permanence had been established. Out of the successive migratory waves from the east that led to a thorough mixing of the various tribes, of which only a few retained their names (the Chatti and the Frisii, for example), larger folk groupings had formed, and because the ancient ties of blood had loosened another factor came to provide the feeling of belonging together. Consanguinity was superseded by the tie that binds human beings to the soil they till. Belonging to a locality became synonymous with belonging to a clan. The village community was born. Individuals were no longer bound together by ties of blood but by the feeling that they were united with the soil.'[20] Thus there came about the transition from ties of consanguinity to the feeling of belonging to the soil; though of course the importance of consanguinity remained for a long time and continued to be a major factor at the foundation of social life.

On the other hand we have to take into account the inner structuring of the Germanic peoples into the estates. The significance and caste-like rigidity of the estates is also connected with the evolutionary stage of the sentient soul, as Hans Erhard Lauer pointed out.[21] We hear that the Saxons, a very conservative Germanic people, maintained estates of a caste-like character well on into the eighth century until shortly before they were conquered by Charlemagne. A modern historian points out: 'The Saxon estates were more rigidly separated than in any other Germanic people of the continent. The clearest expression of this is the fact that intermarriage between them was forbidden or punished by death, and in other areas there were similarly sharp demarcations. A Saxon estate was almost a caste.'[22]

These castes or estates were originally, and to a considerable extent continued to be, communities bound by consanguinity. Out of all these communities founded on the ties of blood - and gradually replacing them - there grew over the centuries all manner of other associations which then became the bearers of medieval social life, giving it that particularly Germanic and then specifically German slant. There were the craft associations and the trade associations, and associations concerned with the cultural life; all kinds of structures that grew organically, no 'state' but situations of human beings belonging together. These were the particularly

Germanic and then German ways in which the ego lives. It is an ego that does not shut itself off from other egos but rather one that joins together with others so that notwithstanding a defiant struggle for freedom the single individuals incline towards one another and work together to bring about many and varied forms of legal entity. The sense of belonging is everywhere, arising not out of any sacrifice of personal striving but out of a voluntary adaptation to a society that is full of life.

*

An important aspect of the migration of the Germanic peoples was discussed by Rudolf Steiner in connection with certain specific dangers coming from the Ahrimanic powers threatening the Roman Empire and Rome from within. We have shown[23] that these powers wanted to turn the Roman Empire into an enormous state machine, a mechanical state. They would have crushed every aspect of life and killed every form of individuality, both that of single human beings and that of folk groups. We have also shown that Roman history as such represented a battle against those powers of rigidity and that the whole personal feeling life of the Romans, all their egoism and emotional strength, was pitted against these powers. On its own, said Rudolf Steiner, this would have been insufficient because the Christianity taken up by Rome would have been distorted into something which would all the more have led to the achievement of Ahriman's aims: the mechanization of culture in modern times.

Then, however, a new force was set against Ahriman, and this consisted in the wave upon wave of the Germanic migrations: 'The opposition against the Romans brought about by the waves of migrating Germanic peoples prevented the rigid mechanization of an all-embracing Roman Empire. You will only understand what happened during the great migration of the Germanic peoples if you see it as an attack against the mechanization of an all-embracing Roman Empire. Everywhere the migration of these peoples pushed its way into the Roman Empire not in order to rid the world of Roman history but in order to push back the powers of Ahriman working behind Roman history, and which, indeed, Roman history itself sought to combat.'[24]

This is understandable when you consider the youthful freshness of the Germanic peoples. They had retained the purer forces of childhood, something that belonged to the pristine original state of humanity and was thus not very accessible to the forces of seduction. The Romans themselves experienced the Germanic peoples in this way. By their very nature the

Germanic tribes were the antithesis of any centralized might of the state, for they lived in diametrically opposite social impulses. They were thus an effective counterforce to the Ahrimanic tendencies of the Romans; the forces of death were confronted by the bubbling life of youth.

The Germanic peoples then proceeded to absorb the Greco-Latin culture, thus fulfilling a historical law whereby 'older, more spiritual streams of cultural evolution that have lost their youthful vitality though not their spiritual power, are carried forward by younger forces that arise from within the nature of humankind.'[25] (A similar process of 'rejuvenation of the life of spirit' had been at work within a rather smaller evolutionary cycle in the fourth century BC when the still youthful forces of the Macedonians met the mature, more southern Hellenistic stream, which the unused forces of the Macedonians, through the deeds of Alexander, then spread in all directions and transformed into a world-wide cultural factor.)

In another connection Rudolf Steiner juxtaposed the Germanic peoples with the Mongolians; the Huns had given the initial impetus to the migration of the peoples, and in the person of Attila they impinged in a significant way on the history of the Germanic element.

Steiner began by describing the Germanic, or rather the Norman-Germanic social constitution that developed unhindered over a very long time in England. In Russia, too, before the Mongolian invasion, the Normans had had a decisive influence on social structures: 'The Norman-Germanic element rested on the view that . . . closer blood ties must have certain consequences with regard to inheritance . . . The social structure governing inheritance was based on the clan and the super-clan, the closer family and the next-higher grouping. This led to the "prince" who dominates the lower grouping that spreads out beneath him. This is a social configuration arising out of a particular configuration of consanguinity.'[26]

This arrangement is entirely contrary, on the one hand, to the Roman legal and political set-up that organizes everything in an abstract way in accordance with contracts rather than blood ties. Another thing that could never have arisen out of the Norman-Germanic nature if it had been left to itself is a state concept involving a monarchy; nowhere in Europe would such a thing have come about. The Norman-Germanic element by itself would have led only to an organization of society founded on clans or family groupings which would have been relatively individual and autonomous, though united in certain respects under a prince who would have had control of the super-clan.[27] The monarchic concept of the state 'comes from the same quarter as the Mongols'; it came to Russia

8

with the Mongolian invasion and to regions further to the west even earlier.

Behind the Mongols we have to look for the Mongolian element of late Atlantis, of which even the name of Attila reminds us. One source of the monarchic principle as it arose in the Europe of the Germanic peoples, and also in Russia, may be sought directly in Atlantis with its powerful priest-kings.[28]

In addition to this there was an even more direct influence from Atlantis that lived on in the Germanic peoples. We have mentioned the Nibelungen (p.3) whose very name points back to Nifelheim or Nebelheim, the land of mists of northern Atlantis.[29] One Germanic tribe in particular expressly derived its ancestry from Atlantis and saw itself as descending from the Nibelungen, and that was the tribe of the Franks whose sense of rulership is described above. We shall discuss this again later.[30]

The Franks were noteworthy in another sense as well. Of all the Germanic peoples, they came closest to the Roman element, so that they could almost be called the 'Romans' among the Germanic tribes. They adopted Athanasian Christianity from the beginning and founded political structures that lasted for centuries. In Boniface the Frankish Carolingians were protecting the Roman Church as it spread through Germany. Charlemagne re-established a part of the Roman Empire and was crowned Roman emperor by the Pope.

Rudolf Steiner stated[31] that the Germanic peoples of Europe were originally guided by a single archangel. Later they then gradually came to be guided by a variety of archangels as they developed into very different individual folk groups. From among these archangels emerged the leading time spirit of our fifth post-Atlantean era after having received his 'education' from the Greek time-spirit, who had become the leading spirit of exoteric Christianity, and from the archangel of the Romans, who had similarly risen to become a kind of time-spirit.[32]

These supersensible facts provide the spiritual archetype for what happened in external history: The originally homogeneous Germanic element gradually differentiated into several more independent groups. In the fifth post-Atlantean era this element has now become the bearer of culture, but for this to happen there had to be that synthesis of Greco-Roman culture with Christianity and all that the Germanic peoples had to offer. It was this synthesis that gave the Germanic-Roman culture of the Middle Ages its particular stamp. In its youth the Germanic element had to absorb the existing culture and impulses of mankind before being able to awaken fully to an awareness of its own mission.

Rudolf Steiner saw two distinct phases in this process. The first was that of the Germanic soul that spread far and wide in the world. As though through the vanguard of Goths, Lombards and Vandals this Germanic soul element was offered up almost like a sacrifice to the peoples of the west and the south. In the second phase, beginning as early as the ninth century, the spirit began to flash forth out of the Germanic soul element. This spirit became ever more distinct and led, for example in German mysticism, to the uniting of the human soul with God.[33] The German spirit is born out of the Germanic soul element. Out of its soul aspect the human ego awakens to full consciousness of its own individual being stemming from the world of divine spirit.

THE MIDDLE AGES

1. *General Characteristics of the Middle Ages*

We shall approach the social structures and phenomena of life in the Middle Ages by beginning with a general characterization of medieval life and times in the manner already attempted with regard to the whole of the Greco-Latin era.[1] What we have said in that connection is for the most part valid with regard to medieval times as well, since by far the larger part of the Middle Ages fell within the overall Greco-Latin or fourth post-Atlantean era which lasted from 747 BC until AD 1413. Only the very end of the Middle Ages came within the beginning of the fifth post-Atlantean era.

It will be difficult for any historical study of insufficient depth to grasp why spiritual science sees the Middle Ages and Antiquity as belonging to the same overall era. The fundamental and profound differences, even contrasts, between Greco-Roman Antiquity and the Christian-Germanic-Roman Middle Ages are so obvious and blatant that considerable effort is required in order to find what they have in common, what it is that makes of them the totality known as the Greco-Latin era. This totality is founded in the deeper impulses of that era and is especially connected with the fact that, throughout that time, one and the same element of the human being was evolving, namely the intellectual or heart-mind soul, and that this was taking place under the same spiritual influences coming from the cosmos, those belonging to the sign of Aries. In the following, in addition to what is discussed in Volume One, this overall character of the Greco-Latin era will begin to emerge more strongly.

The deep-seated difference between the two main parts of the fourth post-Atlantean era, Antiquity and the Middle Ages, is closely bound up with the fundamental character of the age. It is not only that in its very form it should be divided into two parts, giving it the dual character that befits the intellectual or heart-mind soul.[2] This dual character of the Greco-Roman-Medieval era came about because the central event of human evolution as a whole took place within it, making it the turning point of that evolution. The entry of the Christ-impulse into human evolution, the appearance of God on earth and his passage through death made of this whole era the era of the Incarnation. Its first half lasted until that central event - and in a way for several centuries beyond it owing to a kind of law of inertia. In this first half blossomed the wondrous culture of Antiquity. The Mystery of Golgotha then brought in impulses that gave the whole of human evolution, and thus also the middle era of this evolution - the fourth post-Atlantean era - an immense change of direction which in turn determined the second half of the era and gave the Middle Ages their own particular stamp.

Let us look at the difference between the two halves of the Greco-Latin era from the point of view of the particular element of the human being that was evolving throughout that time, namely the intellectual or heart-mind soul. Without distorting any of the myriad facts it is possible to say that during the first half of the era, the period of Greco-Roman Antiquity, it was primarily the intellectual aspect, the more outward-looking side, of this element that underwent development, whereas during the second half of the era, the Middle Ages, the heart-mind aspect, the more inward-looking side, developed. There is a deep connection between the character of the fourth, middle, post-Atlantean era and the fact that the element of the human soul evolving throughout that time is the only such element to possess these dual aspects that are reflected in its double-barrelled name. Greco-Roman Antiquity saw the birth of clear, intellectual thought in Greek philosophy, and this capacity was then applied practically and soberly to the arrangements of Roman law and the structure of the state. The Germanic, Christian world of the Middle Ages, on the other hand, brought with it inward-looking, heartfelt reverence. The genuine Christian piety of the Middle Ages showed the relationship of the human heart and mind to the spiritual world and to Christ. The medieval Scholastics achieved a fine and sublime honing of human thinking and human understanding which remained, however, filled with profound forces of the heart. The kind of logic native to the intellectual or heart-mind soul is not yet the cold, sharp intellect of the consciousness soul we know today. Clarity of thought and warmth of heart and mind are in balance in the intellectual or heart-mind soul, and the best way to study this is by looking at the Middle Ages. With their scholastic capacity for clear thought the educated classes strove to find concepts and intellectual justifications for the same world of Christian revelation that lived in a pure and naïve form in the hearts of the broad mass of the medieval population. Both aspects, the heartfelt piety and the clarity of thought, are wonderfully combined in the architecture, sculptures and pictorial expressions of Gothic cathedrals.

The pre-Christian evolution of Greco-Roman Antiquity led human beings out into the sense-perceptible world that surrounded them horizontally on all sides. The Greek temple is an expression of this. Then came the great change of direction of the fourth post-Atlantean era brought about by the impact of the Christ-impulse. Throughout the Middle Ages human evolution was governed by the vertical aspect.

This came to expression in many ways, indeed in all the great phenomena of the age. Rudolf Steiner described, for the course of human evolution, a succession of three archetypal figures each of whom were the leaders in their time. In ancient days the sons of the gods came down from the heavens; in Grecian times, when the horizontal aspect just described was prevalent, the leaders were wise human beings; and in the Middle Ages, after the impact of the Christ-impulse that turned all human striving to a vertical direction going upwards from below, the saints were regarded as the leaders.[3]

This change of direction in human endeavour, the turning of people's yearning 'upwards', is expressed in works such as Augustine's *City of God*, which throughout the Middle Ages exercised a profound influence on the thoughts and feelings of the western Christian population. Almost at the end of the whole work Augustine has impressive words to say about that higher realm to which the city of god is meant to lead people: 'There we shall be still and see, shall see and love, shall love and praise. Behold what shall be in the end without end! For what else is our end, except to reach the kingdom which has no end?'[4]

The fundamental mood of the dawning Middle Ages thus came to be a yearning for the beyond. It drew people's feelings upwards. Later it found special expression in the cult of the Madonna that so filled people's hearts and minds and souls.[5]

Another expression of this upward endeavour was the logical, Aristotelian philosophical art of the medieval Scholastics and, so akin to this, Gothic architecture with its soaring buildings.

The same change of direction is expressed in the considerations of the Scholastics regarding external, political life and their questions as to the purpose and meaning of society. For Aristotle the purpose of political life had been the achievement of a life of virtue as human beings in the world,[6] which was a 'horizontal' way of looking at things. His great successor among the medieval Scholastics, Thomas Aquinas, the 'prince of the Scholastics', saw the life of the state purely as a means for achieving the much higher and actual purpose of human society, which was to enter into the enjoyment of God through virtuous conduct.[7] This is a 'vertical' way of thinking and feeling.

13

The horizontal line of Antiquity and the vertical line of the Middle Ages together characterize the Greco-Latin era in its totality. Together they form the cross that was set up on Golgotha in this era.

*

Three elements combine and mingle to form the wonderfully homogeneous culture of the Middle Ages: the cultural heritage of Greece and Rome, Christianity in the form of the Roman Church, and the youthful Germanic peoples.

Initially, towards the end of Antiquity, the Christian Church itself absorbed infinitely much of the cultural heritage of Greece and Rome. Later on, both Christianity and the cultural heritage of Antiquity were taken up by the youthful Germanic peoples. They received it all from the hands of the Roman Church which constituted a cultural force of immeasurable significance for the Middle Ages. The Church became the teacher of these peoples, rearing them throughout the centuries of the Middle Ages during which they passed through their youthful stage while they were preparing for their actual mission, on which they were not to embark until the fifth post-Atlantean era. In this sense the term 'the Middle Ages', which at first appears to be no more than a formal designation, achieves a deeper meaning. The Middle Ages stand in the middle between the past high culture of Antiquity and the new culture of the consciousness soul which these peoples are to create in the fifth post-Atlantean era.

Because the culture-bearing peoples of the Middle Ages were passing through their youthful stage there was great emphasis on a particular characteristic of the intellectual or heart-mind soul, namely, the fundamental importance of the role played by authority.[8] In the two main sections of life, the religious and spiritual area and the more political and earthly area, people looked up to two great authorities, the Pope and the Emperor. Under the care of these two authorities the youthful peoples of the Middle Ages matured. From these highest authorities, at least in theory, descended the lesser authorities, both sacred and secular, that each higher echelon enjoyed over the next lower section entrusted to it.

*

The whole era of Greece and Rome together with the Middle Ages is that of the Incarnation. The Greeks sought the spirit in the sense-perceptible world, incorporating it, for example, in their sculptures. Christ,

14

the divine spiritual being, incarnated in the human, earthly body of Jesus of Nazareth. Thus, throughout the whole era the spirit was sought in the external world and in the external world the spirit. Hand in hand with this went an important trait: As time went on people became less and less inclined to comprehend anything that was purely spiritual, while on the other hand all sense-perceptible things appeared to be filled with elements of spirit or soul, seeming to show to human beings a perceptible aspect of the spirit.

Thus it was possible for an individual such as Augustine, and indeed the Middle Ages as such, to see in the external Church the undeniable form embracing the supersensible Christian concept of grace, which meant that a whole era could become convinced of the truth of the words *nulla salus nisi intra ecclesiam* (no safety except within the Church). This is why later on the 'Holy Roman Empire of the German Nation', consecrated by its Christian content and clothed in its indispensable form, could become so sacred to people's pious feeling. In the same vein each individual, a being of spirit and soul, a craftsman, for example, confronted the external work he did with his own hands. In his own external work (not, as yet, mechanized by machines) he saw the incarnation of his own spirit and soul and of his own heart forces. The external world of work was filled with soul and, on the whole, human beings found the soul only in connection with the external work they did.

2. Augustine and Charlemagne

St Augustine of Hippo (354-430) and Charlemagne (768-814) are the two figures who most strongly influenced the thoughts and aspirations of the Middle Ages in the realms of social and political life. What came from them represented the ideal according to which the external life of society should be shaped. It goes without saying that reality never quite comes up to the ideal or sometimes even turns into its opposite, but the ideal can nevertheless teach us most about the underlying driving forces, the hopes and ambitions, of an age.

With his great work about the city of God, *De civitate Dei*, Augustine represented rather more the Roman element, the theory of medieval social life, while Charlemagne stood more strongly for the Germanic element and the practical side of things. It may be said that Augustine's book mightily influenced the way people thought and felt about the nature and purpose of secular, political society for a thousand years. Charlemagne, on the other hand, was the most important and influential princely figure who enjoyed the highest reputation throughout the Middle Ages. By being attributed to him, all manner of institutions and laws were justified or made to seem justifiable. Even during his lifetime, but especially in later centuries, legends about the figure of the great emperor abounded, a sure sign of how much he meant to people. Throughout the centuries of the Middle Ages Charlemagne's image stood as the image of the ideal prince.

In *De civitate Dei* Augustine depicted history and the political life of society in the light of the highest ideals of his view of Christianity. Cosmic events in the evolution of the spiritual universe were for him the cause of earthly happenings in history and political life. His starting point was the battle of cosmic powers and the fall of the human race.

The company of angels - so said Augustine - split long ago into those who were good and those who were evil and filled with pride. There arose in consequence two invisible societies in the spiritual world, that of the elect and that of the damned. The prince of the evil angels seduced the first pair of human beings, thereby gaining great influence for the evil society on earth, so that the evil society became earthly in contrast to the heavenly society. Through Christ, the central figure of world history, the 'order of love', which had been destroyed by the seduction of human beings, was re-established, and through Christ the city of god was brought back to the earth despite the fall of man, so that now, inextricably intermingled, both states exist side by side until the last judgement. Both are present in the invisible and the visible world. The earthly city consists of the evil angels and the evil human beings. The evil angels influence events on the earth and the citizens of the earthly city seek pleasure through earthly goods and thus lack peace. Christ, however, the second ancestor, creates through grace a nation of those who live in reconciliation and love God. In a community of peace with the good angels this nation founds the city of God on the earth. This city, however, does not belong to the earth but to heaven. It is founded on the love of God and the disregard of self, whereas the earthly city is founded on the love of self and the disregard of God. Tyranny holds sway in the latter, while in the former each serves the other in love. Cain is the founder of the earthly city. However, the political realm must not be entirely confused with the earthly city of evil because the heavenly city brings holiness to the political realm. Every union founded on bonds of love belongs by its very nature to the heavenly city and comes from God. Such a union is the family, through which God endeavours to counteract the disunity of human beings. Another such union is the political unity of the state; it, too, comes from God, as do the authorities; and the princes are predestined by God to be the rulers. The history of the world that is evolving through this battle will come to an end when the number of the citizens of heaven is achieved.[1]

Since human beings consist of body and soul they need to participate in secular society as well as in the kingdom of God. The aim of secular society is peace on earth, which Augustine described as the union or concord of wills. The principle of justice must hold sway so that the secular regime can fulfil its aims with regard to human beings, the earth and the times. These justified aims become distorted, however, if the state regards them as divine and sets them up as the highest, for then secular society becomes *civitas terrena* (the earthly city) in the evil sense. Everything intended for the good must point upwards and be filled with the spirit, for, without justice, what are kingdoms except great robber bands?[2] In the city of God the love of God becomes an immediate social bond; in God, the *bonum commune* (the general good) of *De civitate Dei*, earthly contradictions lose their sharpness.[3]

Secular and political society is thus for Augustine merely a means whereby human beings can be led towards perfection in the Christian sense, as he understood it and as it lived in him. In humility and piety it is therefore the task of the leader of the state to guide it in such a way that it becomes a part of the city of God and his subjects citizens of God. To this end his appointment comes from God.

As we know from Einhard, Augustine's *De civitate Dei* was Charlemagne's favourite work. His reign constituted an endeavour to realize the thoughts it expressed. With his conquests he founded a great kingdom such as had not existed in the west since the demise of the Roman Empire. The idea of the Roman Empire as a universal, political kingdom still lived in people's minds and Charlemagne's conquests gave it new life, although on a considerably smaller scale. In the sense of the city of God he intended it to provide the outer vessel for the great spiritual unification of western humanity in the Roman Christian faith. Thus arose the universal monarchy based on the Christian hierarchy with its perfect union of Church and secular rule. As well as being a secular prince, Charlemagne was also something like a high priest, *pontifex in praedicatione*, as Alcuin put it. He saw himself to be a defender of the faith and lord of the Church in the service of God. He described his task to Leo III in AD 796 by saying that it was his duty, with the help of the divine powers, outwardly to defend with weapons the holy Church of Christ against pagan attack and destruction by unbelievers, and inwardly to strengthen it by giving recognition to the Catholic faith. The same view was expressed in the *Libri Carolini* written at his behest and published under his name in AD 790.

Charlemagne's concept of his relationship, as a prince, with God found expression in his use of the devotional formula *gratia Dei* (by the grace of God) which appears regularly in his earlier documents and which shows that he regarded his kingship to be in the service and by the grace of God for the temporal and eternal welfare of his subjects. Previously this devotional formula had been used for a long time by the Church, so its adoption by a secular ruler is significant as regards his fundamentally theocratic impulse. The historical background to this will be discussed in the following from other points of view.

The above descriptions of Augustine's city of God and of Charlemagne have dwelt more on the ideal aspects of each. Another aspect was discussed by Rudolf Steiner[4] when he pointed out that Augustine 'takes up the Christ concept but constructs the state in such a way that it becomes the Roman state. He includes Christ in the idea of the state suggested to him by the Roman state.' It must indeed be conceded that Augustine was deeply related to what motivated the Romans. After Peter he was the next greatest inaugurator of Roman Christianity, and from this Roman Christianity many threads lead directly to the present day:

Look, for example, at the Council of Constantinople in AD 869; its 'abolition of the spirit' lives on in modern body-soul psychologies. The thinking developed by the medieval Scholastics likewise lives on in modern science that applies this thinking solely to a single field, that of the physical world. Steiner frequently pointed to this, for example in a lecture on 8 June 1920 in Stuttgart, in which he also revealed another seemingly paradoxical link: 'Where is the final outcome of medieval Catholic scholastic thought? Where is the final outcome of the social view expressed in Augustine's *City of God* and what came after it, that rigid organization, that military order of human society? The final outcome of medieval scholastic theology as regards its thought forms is Marxism. This is what is being prepared today as socialist teaching for the broad masses of the population. . .'[5]

Charlemagne, too, was deeply related to this Roman element, apart from an Atlantean heritage also present in him which we mentioned above. Not without reason was Augustine's *De civitate Dei* his favourite work. With Roman methods, with the external force of the sword, he spread 'Christianity', among the Saxons, for example, using his usual bloody tactics. He conquered his kingdom in the Roman spirit, making use of Christianity as a political force. He 'made use of the Church in order to extend his territory. And the task of the bishops he set up in power was in most cases that of being a tool serving his rule . . .'[6]

Augustine and Charlemagne stand before us as the most important exponents of that phase of Christianity, a Christianity darkened by the continuing historical might of all that the Roman Empire had stood for and yet broadened by it to become a cultural factor of the greatest dimensions.

3. The Holy Roman Empire of the German Nation

The three elements of medieval cultural life mentioned earlier,[1] - the heritage of Antiquity, Christianity, and the world of the Germanic peoples - are all revealed impressively in the figure of Charlemagne. These same elements are also present *per excellence* in the 'Holy Roman Empire of the German Nation'. By being a *Roman* Empire it harked back to Roman Antiquity, the old *imperium romanum*. This was to be continued in a *holy* Roman Empire in such a way that it reckoned with the world-impulse of Christianity and wanted to serve it as a vessel serves its content. All of this, finally, was to be done by the *German Nation* that had gradually formed out of the youthful Germanic peoples.[2]

What emerges here is a historical stream coming up northwards from the south in the middle between east and west.[3] In its deeper sense it is a stream of the human ego. It is connected with a mission of law founded on the human ego. In pre-Christian times this was borne by the Romans and after the advent of Christianity was to be taken up by the Germanic peoples who were now to be the bearers of the developing human ego. A vocation of external, imperialistic rulership was not meant by this but rather one founded on a Christian principle of peace and order bearing Christian impulses and spreading through the world from central Europe. What grew instead out of the endeavours to create the Holy Roman Empire of the German Nation was described by Rudolf Steiner as something that had been 'superimposed' on to the German element, namely a factor that was all-too Roman. Someone wishing to comprehend the underlying forces of history would have to 'recognize the universal ideal of the medieval empire as the unfree precursor of a future free human goal'. This was Karl Christian Planck's description of the underlying facts with which we are here concerned.[4] It thus becomes clear that with regard to that strangely mixed formation known as the Holy Roman Empire of the German Nation we have to distinguish between three manifestations: what came as Roman heritage from the past, its Roman Catholic manifestation in the Middle Ages and, finally, its task for mankind as a whole pointing on into the future. This task is closely akin to the central European, German element and calls for capacities and methods that no longer have any connection with the Roman past in a wider sense.

*

Let us turn briefly to a consideration of past aspects of the concept of an empire, or imperialism. In characterizing the great 'imperialisms' of history Rudolf Steiner once described the stage to which the medieval empire, the German *imperium*, belonged as one occurring in the 'second phase'.[5] Initially, above all in the Orient, there had been the great empires of Asia, of which ancient Egypt had been a derivation. Characteristic of this phase had been the ancient Persian and especially the ancient Assyrian empire. Here the ruler had also been the god working in physical reality. Ministers and courtiers had been divine beings, higher than ordinary mortals through having been schooled in the Mysteries. In this phase of 'imperialism' the spiritual world had been reality; it had been directly present in earthly arrangements of rulership.

In a later, second phase the ruler was no longer regarded as a god but as one sent or inspired by God, and filled with the divine. The soul realm alone was affected by this. External arrangements of rulership became merely an image, a symbol of spiritual, divine order. For instance the external Church represented an image of the heavenly hierarchies in the sense described by Dionysius the Areopagite. This was the second phase, that of symbols or tokens of reality. Church communities and secular communities came into being. Augustine's *City of God* belongs here, too, as does the medieval empire superimposed on the German people as the Holy Roman Empire of the German Nation. Everything was symbolic of the divine, spiritual realm; the ruler ruled 'by the grace of God'. He was no longer divine but he signified the divine.

Finally Rudolf Steiner also described a third phase of 'imperialism' as having developed in our own time, in which what comes from souls on earth is no longer even a symbol, having become nothing more than empty phrases. In the first phase external arrangements of rulership had been spiritual reality; in the second they became symbols of the spirit; and in the third everything used to adorn real external arrangements of power has become an empty phrase. The fact that now everything has become an empty phrase does mean, however, that there is a space waiting to be filled with a new kingdom of the spirit, a completely new kingdom.

The Holy Roman Empire of the German Nation belongs to the second of these three phases. It was a whole network of symbols which did not lead to a full spiritual reality because the churches prevented this from happening. It was possible only to swim or float about in spiritual reality among the many half-understood aspects that appeared and disappeared like the sunlight streaming in through the stained-glass windows of medieval churches. People recoiled from clear, sharply-defined comprehension. In the social realm, as well, everything was unclear and ill-defined. The Holy Roman Empire of the German Nation lasted until 1806, but in the end there was no meaning whatever left behind the symbols.[6]

For many centuries the symbolism of the medieval German empire culminated in the coronation of the emperor,[7] and akin to this was the symbolism of the king's coronation in many countries. In Britain this has been retained very impressively right up to our present time and has thus become a relic of the second phase of 'imperialism' still at work in the third phase.

Dante became the great herald of the Holy Roman Empire in the Middle Ages. In *De monarchia* he saw 'oneness' as the root of 'goodness' and 'manifoldness as the root of evil'.[8] He was fully in favour of the Roman Empire and used the methods of Scholasticism to prove the right of the Romans to dominate the world. Rudolf Steiner described Dante, that outstanding figure of his time, as finding it perfectly in order to justify the fundamental right of the Romans to conquer the whole world by citing, among other things, the fact that Aeneas, the ancestor of Rome, won the right to rule Asia through his marriage to the Trojan woman Creusa, Africa through his marriage to Dido, and Europe through his marriage to Lavinia.[9]

Speaking about the Holy Roman Empire and Dante in another connection Rudolf Steiner said: 'For the Holy Roman Empire was to a large extent founded on ideals. If you do not wish to believe other sources which speak of these ideals, then read Dante's *De monarchia*, or investigate what else Dante thought about these things. Consider, for instance, that it was Dante who reproached Rudolf von Habsburg for taking too little care of Italy, "the most beautiful garden in the Empire"! Dante was, at least during that part of his life which matters most, an ardent adherent of that ideal community which had come into being and was called Germany-Italy.'[10]

In the way it lived beyond its time - that is, beyond the fourth post-Atlantean era - the Holy Roman Empire of the German Nation is closely linked with something that has been called the 'spectre' of Roman times.[11]

Having made this statement, Rudolf Steiner continued: 'Until 1806 the Holy Roman Empire of the German Nation dragged on, a more or less real, more or less nominal entity. It was 1806 before it disappeared, only it did not actually disappear, for it was pushed into something else. This Holy Roman Empire that had for so long more or less successfully held together or divided all kinds of peoples, this imperial impulse of the Holy Roman Empire of the German Nation in fact merely passed over into the reign of the House of Habsburg.' It was transferred to the state of Austria-Hungary that covered various nations as though with a mantle under the rule of the House of Habsburg. It was something profoundly medieval, for it was nothing other than imperialism as it had been under the old Holy Roman Empire of the German Nation. Rudolf Steiner contrasted this with something entirely modern, namely the imperialism of the Hohenzollerns in Prussia. He called this: Americanism within the German character and world.[12]

4. Medieval Universalism

In Book 1 of *De monarchia* ('Concerning the need for a monarchy') Dante argued: Everything is best arranged when it is in harmony with God's purpose. It is God's purpose that every creature should resemble God as far as is in keeping with its own nature. 'Therefore the human race is best served when it as far as is possible resembles the image of God. The human race is most like God when it is most highly united . . . Joined together under a single prince, mankind thus has the greatest likeness with God.' Universal monarchy is in keeping with God's purpose.[1]

Behind a train of thought and logical argumentation such as this stands the spiritual reality of medieval universalism.

Christianity is intended for mankind as a whole; and out of its own inner necessity the ancient Roman Empire likewise became a supranational, universal structure. Despite all their contrasts and differences, these two universal impulses found one another and joined together. The universal Roman Empire became a kind of vessel whose content was universal Christianity. This was how human hearts and minds regarded both the ancient Roman Empire and its successor, the Holy Roman Empire, for many centuries.

Novalis, too, in his hymn to these centuries, 'Christianity or Europe', described this medieval universalism: 'Wonderful, shining times were they when Europe was a single Christian land, when a single Christianity inhabited this continent in human form, when a single common cause united the most distant provinces of this wide and spiritual kingdom . . .'

So what people could appear more suited to be the political leaders serving this medieval impulse of universality than the German people, who had always been universal in themselves because they bore within them the germ of the ego, the central element of mankind; the German people who venerated as their leading spirit the archangel Michael, warrior for Christ, and who carried his image on their imperial banner as the token of their armies, for example in the battle against the Hungarians by the river Lech in AD 955?

The medieval empire of the Germans is only understood aright when it is seen as arising out of the task the German people performed 'for the world as a whole' on the basis of their relationship with the human ego, just as, out of their intellectual-soul forces, again in accordance with the medieval universal view, the French took care of the element of *studium generale*, the cultivation of scholastic science 'for the world as a whole', while the Italians, also 'for the world as a whole' cared for the *sacerdotium*, the priestly aspect of the Christian Church. All these things were seen as belonging to mankind as a universal whole. These peoples, each with their own particular God-given gift, appeared united as in a single family, especially these three who all looked up to Charlemagne as their common father.[2]

The overall atmosphere of the time was one of universalism, and this is the basis on which we must seek an understanding of the Roman expeditions and the Italian policies of the medieval German emperors and kings. To apply yardsticks and viewpoints of expediency arising out of much more recent conditions and habits of thought merely betrays a lack of deeper historical comprehension. The German emperors and kings made their way to Italy because this was in keeping with the idea for which they lived, the ideal of a universal *imperium*, and because they desired to fulfil what they regarded as their God-given task of establishing peace and justice in the world. Moreover, the human ego is intensely attracted to the sentient soul and the land in which it was so well developed.

According to Rudolf Steiner 'the ego, with its inward intensity, needs to immerse itself in the sentient soul if it is to be fructified by what comes towards it in the forms of the external world . . . Thus it is only to be expected that human beings belonging to the ego-culture of central Europe will seek a living contact with the culture of the sentient soul in the south. They will seek political expansion in that direction, but also more exalted spiritual relationships.

You need only look at the history of the Staufen dynasty and what was present in the Staufens and Welfs in central Europe. Look at what is said about the continuous expeditions of the Saxon and Staufen rulers to Italy; look at the whole living interplay between central Europe and Italy and you will see an exact picture of the way sentient soul and ego live together.'[3]

The Church with its single supra-national hierarchy, mirror image of the heavenly hierarchy, was universal in character, encompassing all human beings. The German Roman Empire, as we have seen, was also supra-national and universal. In addition to these there were many other communities and associations of a more restricted kind that even so were also universal in character. The orders of knighthood were regarded 'as a universal company modelled on the Church and embracing the whole of the western world'.[4] The powerful free towns with their citizenry, 'whose interests criss-crossed Europe in all kinds of splendid associations, felt themselves to be parts of a European community to which they belonged'.[5]

All this shows that the world of the early and high Middle Ages, with its universalism of culture, politics and an incipient economic system, did not yet have any *national* feelings; it lacked a national consciousness or indeed any kind of nationalism. Only when the medieval world began to crumble did any of this begin to appear. It came when divisions and differentiations took hold as people turned away from the spiritual ideals of the Middle Ages towards the material world of sharp contours and separateness. This was especially the case in the Gabriel age, thus named after its leading time spirit, which began in the first third of the sixteenth century and lasted almost until the end of the nineteenth. The impetus it brought, stemming from the moon, was strongly bound up with the forces of birth and heredity which gave human beings a more external relationship to the outer, physical world.

Obviously the principle of national differentiation that was to succeed medieval universalism began to appear in the west in the later Middle Ages, emanating characteristically enough from the French, a people influenced by those moon forces. Here, as though proclaiming in advance the changes that were to take place in the fifteenth century when the fifth post-Atlantean era began, a symptomatic event occurred at the beginning of the fourteenth century. Rudolf Steiner also saw this as a turning point in modern history: 'It was the pressure exerted by France on the papacy in the year 1303 when the Pope was forced to transfer his residence from Rome to Avignon. This event occurred almost simultaneously with another, in which the order of the Templars, an organization that had a rather extraordinary relationship with the Church, was destroyed and robbed of its wealth by the government of France.'[6] Steiner described these events as turning points because they showed that the medieval idea of universal unity supported by Pope and Emperor alike was beginning to be replaced. Breaches were appearing in the way human beings were organized in relation to one another in the Middle Ages, when there was a sense of belonging to a coherent whole that encompassed all national and other kinds of groups. A new element entered the souls of western human beings, a sense of nationality, and now England and France began to evolve almost as models of what a new nation state should be.[7]

5. The Crusades

The Crusades were intimately bound up with the medieval impulse for a universal Christianity. According to Rudolf Steiner an important initial stimulus came from the wish to work from Jerusalem to overcome Roman Christianity. Of course the Popes were not a party to this aspect, but Godfrey of Bouillon, for example, was. A strengthened, common faith such as lived in Bernard of Clairvaux led to an inclination 'to set Jerusalem in the place of Rome and found an anti-Roman Christianity centred on Jerusalem. This is what actually lay at the foundation of the Crusades. Godfrey of Bouillon was not sent by the Roman Popes. He took up the cause of the Crusades with the purpose of establishing in Jerusalem a bulwark against Rome in order to make Christianity independent of Rome. This was an idea that held sway for several centuries. Henry II, the Saint, expressed it as an *ecclesia catholica non romana*'.[1]

'Godfrey of Bouillon . . . actually intended to conquer Jerusalem in order to establish a counter-balance against Rome. Neither he nor his companions spoke about this openly, but in their hearts they bore the call to battle: "Jerusalem against Rome".'[2]

Steiner also described the crusaders setting out for the east in the first instance to discover what sacred relics they might find to which their faith could be attached. They longed for a real link between their faith and the actual events of the Mystery of Golgotha.[3]

In particular they longed to possess the holy sepulchre; it was for the sake of the holy sepulchre that they wanted the Holy Land. They hoped that possession of the Holy Land in which the Redeemer had lived and worked would bring them decisive advantages for the redemption of their souls. This once again is an expression of that fundamental characteristic of the Middle Ages that made people look for the spirit and soul, or for an ideal, in the external world clothed in physical form. However, there was nothing left for the crusaders to find.

Hegel expressed this very profoundly in his *Philosophy of History*: 'Christianity was not to find its ultimate truth in the holy sepulchre. Instead it received once again the answer given to the disciples when they went there seeking the body of the Lord: "Why seek you the living with the dead? He is not here, he is risen." You should not search for the foundation of your religion in the sense-perceptible grave where lie the dead but in the living spirit within you. In the end it has come down to this: The immense idea of the link between the temporal and the eternal has lost any spiritual content, so that the eternal as such is sought in isolated external objects. Christianity is left with the empty sepulchre; it failed to find the link between the temporal and the eternal and thus lost the Holy Land.'[4]

This fundamental error of the crusading western world is also obviously connected in a profound way with the fact that the consequences of the Crusades came to be so diametrically opposed to their origins and intentions. Indeed, they initiated a complete turn-about of the original cultural impetus of the Middle Ages. One of these effects was the introduction of western peoples to the more advanced material culture of the Near East, the outcome of which was a blossoming in the west of secular culture and civilization made possible by the opening up of trade. As a result the towns of Italy, the bearers of this increasingly lively trade, began to flourish, and this led in turn to the increasing importance of town culture as such and all that was later to stem from that.[5] Furthermore, in the Holy Land whence that mighty universal impulse uniting all mankind had come, rivalries began to flash between the western peoples. They began to experience their differences in a consciousness of nationality which in its later, much stronger form was to replace and virtually extinguish the medieval sense of oneness.

Something else was also experienced in the east by the crusaders, which Rudolf Steiner described as follows: 'A tremendous amount changed in Europe as a result of the Crusades, whereas very little of what they had intended actually came to pass. Much was transformed in Europe as a result of what the crusaders met out there in the east, and in addition to this came the acquaintance they made with the whole *phenomenon of the state which had developed much earlier there than in Europe*. The structures of administration were much less formal in Europe before the Crusades than they afterwards came to be. *It was as a result of the Crusades that such extensive regions came to be organized in the form of states.*'[6]

We shall have more to say about these eastern origins and prototypes of subsequent western states, but in the present context we are concerned with way the first beginnings of a sense of nationality on the one hand and of an organized state on the other emerged from the Crusades as a result of the way their original impetus became transformed into something that was its total opposite. Later on, in the early centuries of the fifth post-Atlantean era, both were to be joined ever more closely in the phenomenon of the nation state when it began its triumphal march across western Europe.

6. Dualism. Pope and Emperor

We have repeatedly pointed out the profound duality that underlies the nature of the fourth post-Atlantean era or indeed the nature of the intellectual or heart-mind soul. By the end of the fourth post-Atlantean era two branches of the social organism had reached maturity because the older one, the spiritual life of culture, had been joined by a second one, the independent life of law and politics whose birth had been particularly assisted by the Romans. These two branches came to stand side by side in the Middle Ages in the dualism of Church and Empire, of ecclesiastical life and secular authority, of Pope and Emperor. The greater part of the medieval centuries was taken up with the way these two went along either side by side, together with one another, or one against the other.

The two powers were not clearly distinguishable either in their ideals or, even less, in their practical manifestations. The very fact of their being at loggerheads arose from the similarity of their purposes and aims. Both felt they were the executors of a lofty mission of a universal nature entrusted to them by the spiritual world or God.[1] In order to fulfil this mission both, the Pope just as much as the Emperor, strove to develop their power over the material world. They became, as Rudolf Steiner put it, 'rivals in the battle for external influence. They were two of a kind, working in one direction. At loggerheads with one another were a secular power and a Church that had become secular'.[2]

The aspirations of Pope and Emperor stemmed, of course, from widely different origins and it was only in the course of time that this disparity of origin became blurred. It is important to be aware of this difference because it throws light on the deeper historical purpose of the two streams as well as on their mutual opposition.

The Pope represented the apostolic succession in a Church that had grown ever more 'Roman' in the fourth post-Atlantean era. He also represented the succession of the Roman Caesars, especially as the incumbent of the office of *Pontifex maximus*.[3] Initially he, and not the Germanic kings, was the successor to the Roman Empire. They only assumed this mantle later when the medieval Empire came into being.

The origins of the Emperor's office lie further back in the much more ancient world of Atlantis. We have already mentioned[4] that the Franks regarded themselves as the descendants of the Nibelungen, the inhabitants of *Nebelheim* or the land of mists in the northern regions of Atlantis. It was from their midst that the first Emperor, Charlemagne, emerged.

In a much wider context Rudolf Steiner described the following:[5] Among the Franks, who were so happy to conquer western Europe, there was a dynasty of rulers who traced their origins back to Atlantis. These were the Nibelungen, from which the name 'Ghibelline' arose. An ancient awareness lingered of a dynasty of rulers among the Franks who had their roots in the old land of the Nibelungen where they wielded both priestly and worldly power. That is why Charlemagne wanted to be crowned in Rome, so that a spiritual element could be added to the secular one. Originally all power was derived from what came over from Atlantis.[6] The awareness of a twilight of the gods added a tragic side to the secular ruling dynasty, for it was said that those who were initiated would have to be supplanted by something else. The mood this created was expressed in the Barbarossa legend and something was added that was not usually contained in that legend, namely that Barbarossa was considered to be the continuation of the ancient Frankish dynasty. The Hohenstaufen were the Ghibellines, the Nibelungen.

On the basis of these and other indications given by Rudolf Steiner, Ernst Uehli further maintained[7] that other families, after the time of Charlemagne, who combined greater or lesser power with ownership of land and serfs, were also by their nature descendants of the Nibelungen. In addition to the Staufen dynasty there were thus also the Welfs; both belonged to the Nibelungen stream. While Henry the Lion embodied the wild stubbornness of the Nibelungen, Frederick Barbarossa was a Christian Nibelung. Of him it was said that he set out on his Crusade in order to bring the Holy Grail from the east to the west. Instead he met his tragic end.[8]

This brief summary of these important remarks must suffice in the present context, where they are intended to show that the medieval German ruling dynasties contained something in their disposition that harked back to very ancient and universal origins of a theocratic kind not connected with the papal Church.

These origins do indeed throw a bright light on Charlemagne, the founder of the German Emperorship. We have already said that Augustine's *City of God* was his favourite work and that he conceived of his own Empire as a 'city of God' in the Augustinian sense. Rudolf Steiner pointed out[9] that Charlemagne had felt himself to be guided by the Divinity or by divine powers, and Steiner linked this to what he had mentioned elsewhere[10] about the use of the Carolingian sword in the cause of the Filioque Clause in the Creed (the procession of the Holy Spirit from the Father *and from the Son*),[11] for which the Carolingians had done a great deal more than the Popes. We see from this how strongly this afterglow of the Atlantean priest-kingship entered into the Christian impulse. Steiner pointed out that in a certain sense exoteric and esoteric Christianity were forged together in Charlemagne.[12] This does not mean that the Atlantean origin of the Frankish attitude to rulership is not also an aspect of the first importance, especially with regard to the later bitter battles during the Middle Ages between Emperor and Pope, which can be regarded, as Ernst Uehli said, as battles 'between an Atlantean-Nibelungen rulership and a Petrine-Papal rulership'.

In order to delve more deeply into this universal contrast, Uehli compared the picture of Charlemagne's imperial coronation with another, earlier, image, that of Attila appearing with the Huns before the gates of Rome in the year 452. 'Surrounded by Roman senators and priests, Bishop Leo went out to meet the Hun. Before the face of Attila he invoked the great patron saints, Peter and Paul. Attila, for whom the patronage of protective powers was a perfectly ordinary matter, saw and recognized that protection and retreated. Rome was saved and the reputation of the Roman bishop rose immensely. The Roman Church had won a spiritual battle and knew full well how to make the most of it. By bringing about the retreat of the Huns the Roman bishop had also won a spiritual victory over fading Atlantean spirit powers coming over from Asia. In the Nibelungen-Frankish and later ruling dynasties, however, the Church was faced with fading Atlantean ruling powers that now came up against the Church in a transformed Germanic and Christian guise that could not be conquered in the way the Huns had been.'[13]

We should add that these Germanic, Christian powers of Atlantean origin in addition derived from quite different elements within ancient Atlantis, namely the progressive Atlantean races, whereas the Huns were descended from degenerate Atlantean races. This is a fundamental difference.

It must not be forgotten, though, that in their polemic quarrels with the Pope the Emperors, especially Barbarossa, referred to their own Roman antecedents as well. They sought justification in the Roman Empire of Antiquity for their power which, as an entirely secular power, they considered theirs by right. In doing so they referred back to Caesar Augustus, who was more ancient than the Curia.

Once again we have before us in Pope and Emperor two powers that were too alike, both too 'Roman', to be able to complement one another in harmony.

Thus for centuries the Middle Ages wrestled with the problem of finding a balanced relationship between Pope and Emperor. Images emerged, such as the doctrine of the two swords, the spiritual sword to be wielded by the Church, and the secular sword to be wielded by the power of the Emperor (on behalf of the Church, however, as those on the side of the Church insisted). Another image was the very meaningful one of the sun and the moon, taken from the cosmos.[14] In various ways the Church was compared with the sun and the Emperor and Empire with the moon. Something spiritual was correctly sensed in this image, for in the Church there lived, despite everything, some aspects of the Sun of Christ, and in the *imperium romanum* perpetuated by the Emperor there lived something based on the law belonging to pre-Christian times in which the old moon forces predominated. On the other hand of course the Church was filled with the spirit of ancient Rome while the Empire strove to be a Christian, *Holy* Roman Empire. Thus were the edges blurred. First the Emperors dominated the Popes, and later the power of the Popes predominated. Characteristic of every situation was the mingling of spiritual and secular. The Middle Ages never succeeded in overcoming these contrasts; they never managed to progress beyond the doubtfulness of the duality. In the physical world of space in which duality is valid, doubt reigns supreme. Social dualism cannot overcome it. The doubt that reigned in the dualistic Middle Ages can only be overcome by a threefold understanding and shaping of the world and of the human being, as well as social life as a whole.

7. The Towns

In the Middle Ages, as indeed throughout the whole of the Greco-Latin era, the third branch of the social organism, the economic sphere of commerce and industry, had not yet been 'born', which is to say that people were not yet aware of it as something separate; it still played a subordinate role. To the medieval way of thinking, the economy still functioned, like an embryo, inside the organism of politics and rights. This has been discussed elsewhere[1] in connection with Thomas Aquinas' *De regimine principum*. In considering the way a prince should rule, Aquinas listed not only his legal and moral obligations but also economic tasks, and in doing so he used expressions such as the 'just price' and 'equitable exchange'. This shows how the ideal of brotherliness or fraternity was still seen through the medium of the legal aspect. The economy as a separate branch of the social organism had simply not yet been born.

The seeds of an independent economic life had already been sown, however, in the medieval towns. Over the centuries our modern economic life sprang from these towns.

Rudolf Steiner often spoke from various points of view about the importance of the medieval towns: 'The fruit of what had been prepared during Germanic times came to the fore later on as the right of the individual personality founded solely on its own achievement and competence. This came to expression in the setting up of the towns. Their culture, spreading across the whole of western Europe in the eleventh century, was a most important phenomenon. The towns came into being because those who felt oppressed by the feudal lords sought a place where, undisturbed, they could enjoy the fruits of their own work and personal skills ... The struggles of the towns for independence against the princes and knights are a clear expression of the struggles of the free and independent personality. This had not been the case either in ancient Greece or in ancient Rome ...

'People began to congregate in towns for purely material reasons. They wanted freedom from oppression, and thus initially their activities focussed on utility and material gain.

'In Italy, out of another kind of town life founded on an ancient, dying culture, came that mighty personality of the Middle Ages, the poet Dante. But in the Germanic towns there came first and foremost practical inventions such as the compass or gunpowder, right up to that most important of inventions: the craft of printing . . .'[2]

'In rural areas, on the farms, the causes for dissatisfaction multiplied. It was thus no wonder that the small towns already existing beside the Rhine and the Danube should begin to grow, while new ones were founded as well. From all directions streamed people who could no longer tolerate the rural situation. A population thirsting for freedom brought about this reorganization of society.

'The culture of the towns arose for purely material reasons. Initially, the culture of the Church remained untouched even though many towns evolved in bishoprics and around monasteries. Town culture focussed on anything to do with medieval trade and craftsmanship and with time it led to entirely new conditions.

'It was the urge of the human personality to unfold that brought about the founding of the towns. This was a huge step along the path towards freedom . . .'[3]

'In the earlier Middle Ages people's self-worth was founded on their position in society. They inherited their standing, rank and position from their forebears and lived and worked in the world in accordance with these entirely non-personal attributes that were not consciously connected with the ego. But later, when trade began to expand and new inventions and discoveries were made, consciousness of the ego also spread. External images of this consciousness soul can be found all over Europe in quite specific kinds of town charters and city constitutions. For example in the history of Hamburg it is quite easy to find proof of the way these things evolved historically. The "free town" of the Middle Ages is an external manifestation of the ego-conscious soul wafting through mankind . . . All the demands of more recent times are nothing other than an unconscious expression of the demands of the consciousness soul . . .'[4]

So the old German legal saying 'town air makes you free' expresses a truth that reaches beyond the immediate realm of the sphere of rights. In the Middle Ages the towns were the cradle of the first beginnings of the consciousness soul, and this became ever truer as time went on. In its initial phase the consciousness soul was kindled by ordinary life in the material world; hence the close connection between its awakening and the economic sphere. The town, in addition, is the place where human beings extricated themselves from land and soil, losing to a large extent the old connection between nature and their whole existence in body, soul and spirit. Human beings became self-reliant, dependent on their own inner resources. It was in the town that they came up against inanimate material in trade and craft, especially later on, in the machine age. The town was thus the place where abstract thinking first began to develop, thinking that in dying makes thought hard and intellectual. The first unfolding of the consciousness soul is closely bound up with this process. It is the first phase in the freeing of the self-reliant human personality.

Of course all this only came to a head during more recent centuries, until in our modern 'asphalt culture' the balance finally tipped towards meaninglessness and desolation. In the Middle Ages we can discern only the very first, though decisive, beginnings of that process. Initially, however, the medieval towns enjoyed an exceedingly lively, healthy and vigorous community spirit, a spirit of wholeness, especially in the independent towns of the Empire, that filtered right down to the individual citizen.[5] Richard Wagner's *Meistersinger* illustrates the atmosphere of an independent town such as Nuremberg.

Rudolf Steiner spoke about the spiritual background of the impulses that led to the founding of medieval towns, and he connected these with the legend of Lohengrin, Parsifal's son.[6] Through his own inner development Parsifal achieves the Holy Grail.

'Parsifal shows us how the human being, having set out on a pilgrimage to the higher ego, finds this higher human ego within himself. Lohengrin, on the other hand, shows us how the people of the Middle Ages lived through a powerful phase of human evolution involving the liberation of the human being, the emergence of the personality out of the old social restrictions. In order to understand the connection of this historical event with the legend of Lohengrin we have to know that in the mysticism of every age steps such as this were symbolized by a female figure. That is why even Goethe, at the end of the second part of *Faust*, spoke of the "eternally female leading us upward and on". This must not be taken as something meaningless or trite. It refers to the soul drawing the human being upwards. The soul is nearly always seen as a female principle while the external human being is depicted as being male.

'In the knowledge of the Mysteries it is known that the great leaders of mankind, the initiates, are those who help humanity take a new step in development.[7] Lohengrin is the messenger of the Holy Grail. He appears before medieval consciousness as the great leader and initiate who takes mankind a step further during the middle part of the Middle Ages. He brought the culture of the towns, he inspired the citizenry as they came into being. This is the Lohengrin individuality; and Elsa of Brabant is nothing other than a symbol for the medieval folk soul who is to take a further step of development under the influence of Lohengrin. The legend of this progress in human history is beautifully and movingly portrayed.'

By the question she asks from curiosity Elsa brings about the disappearance of the initiate. This expresses the increasing earthly darkening of consciousness of the people who find their path of development in the towns. Materialism sets in, and only centuries later will this darkened consciousness, that has, however, set human beings free, once more receive a call from the spiritual world, a call for further great changes of consciousness coming from the continuing, though transformed, stream of the Holy Grail.

The fertile seeds of the modern economic realm, as it later grew on capitalist, bourgeois foundations during the centuries of the fifth post-Atlantean era, were certainly sown in the towns of the Middle Ages. The same cannot be said, however, of the modern state. Its roots lie in the territories of the princes who gradually began to organize their states with the help of legally trained civil servants. This tendency was based on the countryside, not on the towns which were often enough engaged in direct dispute with the princes. With regard to the time beginning around the fifteenth century, Rudolf Steiner pointed out the following:

'People in the towns were proud of their individuality and freedom, as may be seen in the portraits that have come down to us from those days . . . But the village communities remained outside. The power of the territorial princes made itself felt. People in the villages who gradually found themselves in opposition to the towns found their leaders among the ones who took their part, or said they would take their part, against the towns. Under the influence of pressure from the surrounding countryside the towns became a part of wider administrative structures that embodied the principles of Roman law. The modern state came into being. It was formed working inwards towards the towns from the surrounding countryside. What conquered the towns from the surrounding countryside was a juridical Latin or Roman element that was beginning to emerge and had indeed grown so powerful that there was no longer any chance for another stream that was struggling to come to the surface among the rural populations. In England and Bohemia, for example, this was the stream of Wycliffe and Huss, and the Bohemian Brethren. None of this managed to take hold. The only thing that really succeeded in gaining the upper hand was the Roman administrative element.'[8]

8. The Reality of the Commune

In modern times great efforts are made to achieve, by means of planning, something that we now lack but which was present in the Middle Ages as a matter of course without the need for any programmes and without any problems. This was a sense of community in human society embracing the greatest and also the smallest circles and constellations.

At one end of this sense of community, its 'cultural pole', stood universalism founded on Church and Christianity and also on the heritage of Antiquity, the common ideal living in the family of peoples in medieval Europe. In the Middle Ages Christ was still felt to be the spirit of mankind as a whole. Christianity shone for every human being like a sun; and as the sun creates order and harmony in the plant world where every plant turns to it as to a common centre, so did the light and warmth of the Christian sun bring about order and harmony, a genuine sense of community, among the peoples of the west. In this universal spiritual life in the Middle Ages, administered by the Church, lay the culturally productive element arising in human souls which added to - and enhanced - what human beings and folk groups anyway brought with them as creatures of the natural world.

Somewhat closer to this 'natural pole', although still inextricably bound up with the cultural pole, was the political unity of these peoples, or of the great majority, within the Holy Roman Empire. This, too, was supra-national and endeavoured to make of Christianity, as it was understood in those times, a unity and ordering of peoples such as is only conceivable on the basis of a mutual spiritual and cultural ideal. Despite all the quarrels, the Empire provided the peoples with a strong experience of community.

Within each folk group there were, in turn, varying degrees of genuine community such as the tribes, the estates, local rural associations and so on. These belonged more in the region of organic communities based on consanguinity such as arise nearer to the natural pole of social life, where they found a more instinctual human togetherness. All this was still a far cry from the social divisions that were to tear the folk groups asunder from within in later centuries. Here too, uniting the estates and associations, the cultural mood cultivated by the Church was the strongest factor, and it used in particular the picture element which is accessible to all. Rudolf Steiner said in this connection:

'Throughout the centuries Christianity endeavoured to immerse human beings in a common cultural life that would make all individuals equal before God . . . Let us not forget that in the Middle Ages, for example, the content of cultural life was couched in a different medium than is the case today. The content of cultural, spiritual life in the Middle Ages was clothed in images, painted and sculpted images that were in the churches where the most exalted prince and the lowest pauper had equal access to them. This cultural, spiritual life united all people from the lowest to the highest.'[1]

In more recent times, the description continues, literature began to take the place of images. Comprehension of imaginative images waned and people sought their culture in literature, in written and printed words. These increasingly took on forms that caused an upper, educated class to arise alongside ordinary proletarian feelings of a more universal kind. This was the origin of the duality of soul in social life that has done more than anything else to create the deep social chasm we now have, with all its terrible consequences in modern times.[2]

The Middle Ages were the era of firm, genuine human community in close-knit as well as more loosely-structured groups, associations, corporations and co-operatives of all kinds that encompassed the individual within a secure background while his consciousness of self was not yet fully awake. There were the blood ties of the family as well as the associations of trade or craft such as the guilds and corporations. There was the village community founded on the soil and there were spiritual associations such as religious brotherhoods and orders, and above all the great structure of the Church itself, filled with pulsating, community-creating life.

There was a long way to go before the individualism inherent in the age of the consciousness soul would begin to appear. Nevertheless the consciousness soul was there, still slumbering, especially in the Germanic peoples who were to be so strongly orientated towards the human ego. It was slumbering while these peoples passed through their sentient soul phase and their medieval heart-mind soul phase.

Historical scientists have much enjoyed discussing whether 'personality' and 'individualism' existed in the Middle Ages. Some said it did not, for example Jakob Burckhardt,[3] who maintained that the character of the individual personality only appeared on the scene with the Renaissance. Others saw this as a kind of slur on the Middle Ages and sought to demonstrate that personalities of individual character had already existed then, pointing, for example, to the great Staufen king, Frederick II, as the 'first modern man on the throne'. They even looked much further back to the likes of St Augustine as he appears in his *Confessions*.

Such discussions remain relatively unfruitful when account is not taken of the great stages of evolution in human consciousness. The main question to ask is the degree to which the experience of individual personality is achieved, on the one hand during the stage of the intellectual or heart-mind soul and on the other during that of the consciousness soul.

Romans were typical representatives of personality at the stage of the intellectual or heart-mind soul.[4] During this stage the characteristics of personality were only just beginning to emerge and the personality was still semi-instinctively submerged in the social community. The Romans experienced their personality through being citizens. Not until the consciousness soul is achieved does the awareness of personality become strong and absolute enough to blow the community apart. Such impulses did not emerge to any great degree in the Middle Ages. They began to appear in the fifth post-Atlantean era, especially in the culture of the Renaissance, as Jakob Burckhardt correctly perceived.

It is true, however, that there are always precursors of any new stage of consciousness, as well as many stragglers still tagging along with the old. Augustine was one of the earliest representatives of the consciousness soul. Similarly, Frederick II of Hohenstaufen can rightly be regarded as possessing an early unfolding of consciousness-soul impulses. In his case this may be specifically connected with the way he was linked to the stream of Arabism which itself was an anticipation of consciousness-soul impulses on a large scale. Nevertheless, when discussing the character of an age it is no good restricting consideration of its cultural impulses to isolated precursors or to the stragglers. What counts is the general situation. The impulses of the consciousness soul did not begin to be felt to any wide extent until the beginning of the fifteenth century, and even then they came in stages, beginning, at least in certain manifestations, with the higher reaches of society, for example the courts of the princes during the Renaissance and the age of absolutism, and only slowly seeping down to the lower levels.

9. Social Structures in the Middle Ages. Not a 'State'

Even the more strictly defined political structures of the Middle Ages, especially earlier on, were not what could be called a 'state' in the modern sense, if by 'state' is meant a rationally constructed body organized in a planned way and functioning, in accordance with administrative rules and regulations, with a certain degree of centralization. Only if, like Keutgen,[1] you consider any form of human community to be a 'state' can you accept such pronouncements as: 'In the beginning was the state', or: 'The state is a direct consequence of the human being.' To stretch the concept of the state in this way is confusing because it leaves out of account the quite different character of earlier forms of human community.

The rulership of the Merovingian kings, or even Charlemagne's kingdom, should not under any circumstances be called 'states' if precise definitions are required.[2] Broadly this continues to hold good for many further centuries with regard to medieval communities. This absence of a state-like character in medieval social structures is not fortuitous and neither should it be regarded as a defect, for it is closely linked with a fundamental characteristic of the Germanic peoples who, as a result of their strongly-experienced feeling for the freedom of the individual, abhorred any kind of rigid state structure or coercion.[3] 'A concept in which the state claims the total subordination of the individual has always been intolerable for the Germans' sense of freedom. The Germanic people were never wholly devoted to the state; alongside and beneath the power of the state they led their own life in their home, in the community, later on in the town, within organizations pledged to peace, or in circles legally bound together to which the state with its powers had no direct or only limited access. From time immemorial individual and society each asserted their rights.'[4]

Here we have one of the most profound differences between the character of the Germanic peoples and that of the Romans, who inclined towards a centralized state. Rudolf Steiner expressed this difference by saying that the Germanic or German people were fundamentally prone 'to regard an informal organization as the ideal'.[5] There is on the one hand an aversion to external pressure from the state, and on the other something positive that must be equally emphasized: In the Germanic or German character lies a genuine aptitude for forming human communities founded on co-operation in the widest sense.[6]

As far as the Middle Ages are concerned a public state-like organization, determining peoples lives, existed only to a small degree. Instead, however, there was the power of tradition which restricted individuals in all kinds of ways, in the realm of the life of rights, for example, particularly by means of the common law that had evolved from customs and traditions. Restrictions of this kind, and socially determined ways of behaving, have their roots in the moral sphere originating either from ancient instinctive spirituality grounded in heredity or from the spiritual and moral supports built into a people by Christianity and the Church.

In so far as medieval people lived within these restrictions that were intrinsic to their lives, in the sense that they belonged to the sentient soul and also the heart-mind soul, there can be no question of any individual freedom such as belongs to the ideal of the consciousness soul of the fifth post-Atlantean era. On the other hand, in so far as Germanic or German people in the Middle Ages kicked against any external coercion operated by the state, they were manifesting a quality of consciousness as to their freedom such as has been virtually lost in more recent centuries. Thus we can understand why Rudolf Steiner contrasted this medieval consciousness of freedom - which had evolved despite all the opposition that gave medieval times the name of the Dark Ages - with the eighteenth century, the century of the Enlightenment, that was hardly even capable of finding a definition for this freedom.[7]

The fact of the matter was that the new development of state and social life that began at the end of the Middle Ages fell very strongly under the influence of the Roman, centralistic idea of what a state should be, which did not concur at all with the Germanic sense of freedom. In their own search for what they considered freedom to be, the leading personalities of the Enlightenment in the eighteenth century accepted this state structure as something given which they did not question. This holds good especially in the case of France. France's history shows particularly clearly the transition from the strongly Germanic social structures of the Middle Ages to the increasingly centralized forms of later centuries, which came about as a result of the French king's victory over the power of the feudal princes and the estates. The same tendency took hold all over Europe as the Roman idea of the state gained ground after the end of the Middle Ages, in some countries to a greater and in others to a lesser extent.

The social order of the Middle Ages, in contrast, was not constructed on logic. It had grown up organically out of all kinds of actual social structures that had come about gradually on the basis of many and varied situations, each with its own inherent laws - ties of consanguinity, links with the soil, associations of craft and commerce (such as guilds and corporations), scholarly institutions and religious orders, secular and ecclesiastical territorial powers and, finally, the widest of all, the powers of the territorial princes. All these many actual arrangements mingled together in the liveliest fashion.[8] The way even smaller groups enjoyed their own freedoms and their own laws was still very much a matter of instinct; indeed, all medieval social structures were inherently instinctive. There was no conscious direction of the way social structures developed or of the way laws came into being on the basis of custom and habit. This befits the phase of development in which the Germanic peoples in Europe at first lived, still dominated by strong elements of the sentient soul. Only gradually was the element of the intellectual or heart-mind soul nurtured into being by the Roman Church.

One element was characteristic of all these social situations, and that was the way they were all founded on the living relationships of individuals with one another. People related to one another on the basis of their individuality. There was as yet no abstract, inhuman, mechanistic element that later made people feel coldly towards an impersonal state. Social structures in the Middle Ages were founded on human morality. An example of this is the way the feudal system as such was based on the human moral force of mutual loyalty that bound liege lord and vassal together. This moral

39

force was the rock on which the feudal system was built, just as in the old Germanic system loyalty had governed the relationship between a leader and his retinue.

This situation has, on occasion, been misunderstood. Thus, in his *Philosophy of History*, Hegel stated that the legendary honesty of the Middle Ages ought, in reality, to be called '*punica fides* or *graeca fides*, since both princes and vassals only practised loyalty and honesty with regard to their own egoism, self-interest and desires.'[9] The point is not, however, the fact that loyalty was constantly being breached, but that it was nevertheless the moral foundation on which the feudal system was built. It would be impossible, in all honesty, to describe the relationship of the individual to the modern, mechanistic state as in any way one of loyalty. But in the Middle Ages loyalty played a decisive role and the importance attached to it is everywhere mirrored in the literature. The fact that disloyalty was a punishable offence confirms the principle of loyalty. It is even expressed in documents of the time, for example in the way a subject was described as *fidelis noster*, 'our trusty servant'.

Loyalty was one pole of the feudal system, the human and moral pole. The other was the relationship people had to the land, to the soil. Land was granted to people, and those receiving such grants increasingly also had to take on related offices or obligations of various kinds. Thus, through the hierarchical system of human relationships, the feudal system linked the land, the sub-human sphere, with God, the supra-human sphere. The peasant lived and worked with the soil; then came the landlord and after him the feudal prince; above him reigned king or emperor, who in his turn regarded himself as a vassal of the Lord. The feudal hierarchy rises from the soil to the heights of heaven, just like the Gothic cathedral.

The social structures of the Middle Ages were filled with the forces of human morality and surrounded by a religious mood, and therefore human beings were able to relate intimately with them and entrust themselves to them in heart and mind. Because in this phase of the heart-mind soul they were able to participate wholeheartedly in the communal life of these structures they did not have to feel that anything was being imposed on them coercively from outside. In this, the era of the Incarnation, they still sensed what was really at the heart of external appearances; they sensed the spirit in outer forms. This changed in the fifth post-Atlantean era when outer forms increasingly lost their inner soul content as a result of mechanistic thought and technology. Human beings were more and more thrown back on themselves; out of their own inner initiative they had to take hold of the consciousness soul. The mechanistic world that repels the human being and throws him back on himself provides the resistance against which the consciousness soul can awaken.

Towards the end of the Middle Ages came the transition from 'feudal government' to 'government by estates'.[10] As the power of the Empire waned the territorial principalities in Germany grew stronger. Within each principality the prince was confronted by the estates: the clergy, the nobility and the citizens. The latter, in particular, became increasingly important as the towns grew in significance. There was still a distinct duality in the structure of prince and estates, especially as they were often at loggerheads. The estates resisted the despotism of the prince, yet together the two formed a united *territorium*. Frequently it was the estates who defended the unity of the *territorium* against the prince's tendency to divide it up, which stemmed from the old Germanic view of the land as private property to be shared amongst one's sons. The dividing up of land in this way played a large role especially in older German history. It bears witness to the absence of any kind of feeling for the state and it served to forge a strong link between the land and the people on the human level.

Thus in Germany the territorial state - now the word 'state' begins to be justified - became the forerunner of the modern state; it became the soil on which the modern state gradually grew over the centuries. In France things developed in a different direction. There the centralized power of the monarch won the day over the differentiating, fragmenting forces of the vassals. In France the monarchy became the bearer of the Roman idea of a centralized state which emerged victorious in accordance with the 'logic' and consistency inherent in French history.

10. Medieval Forerunners of the Mechanistic Age. Arabism

As we have seen, the medieval forerunners of our modern economic sphere - the third sphere of the social organism - were the towns. Similarly the forerunner of the mechanistic element that was to develop and become dominant in the fifth post-Atlantean era was the Arabism of the Middle Ages.[1] The cultural wave of Arabism was profoundly linked with a great historical impulse to which it gave form, namely, the impulse of the year 666 of which, inspired by Ahriman, the intention had been to bring about a premature development of the consciousness soul before humanity, especially the western peoples, had evolved to sufficient maturity.[2] This impulse of the Ahrimanic powers inimical to Christ aimed to cut humanity off from the future development of its higher elements (the spirit-self, the

666

41

life-spirit, and spirit-man). The Christ-impulse worked against this tendency, as did also, in a certain sense, Islam itself, and as a result its worst effects were halted. Nevertheless the consequences were still disastrous enough, one of them especially being the one-sided development of a cold intellect directed towards the sense-perceptible world and leading to a shrivelling of soul life.

The Arab culture of the Middle Ages became the bearer of these impulses and was thus yet another great cultural factor in evolution. It worked hand in hand with the earlier Roman impulse and was to extend some way beyond it. History in general does not have very much to say about this 'Arabism'.

In the context of world history as a whole Rome, 'Romanism' in the widest sense, led to the darkening of the old experience of spirit, to the 'abolition of the spirit' and thus the restriction of people's awareness to a world consisting only of body and soul.[3] The Arab world impulse then took this further, leading to the mechanization that robbed everything of the soul constituent as well - the 'abolition' of the soul. The former culminated predominantly during the fourth post-Atlantean era and the latter, despite its earlier beginnings, during the fifth post-Atlantean era. There is a certain evolutionary logic in the way the second step followed the first.

The great cultural movement of Arabism in the Middle Ages sowed the seed of the mechanistic element among the peoples of the west, as elsewhere. This germinated fully in more recent centuries, especially in western Europe where it enjoyed a strong revival ensuing from the reincarnation of the individuals who had once been its original instigators.

One of the seeds of Arabism that had been sown in the realm of political, social life was the peculiar kind of state that had come into being in Sicily under the influence of the Saracens and then been carried further by the Normans in Sicily and southern Italy. Under Frederick II, the Hohenstaufen Emperor, this was developed even further, and historians and political scientists ever since have described and extolled it as the 'first modern state'.

The type of state that awaited Frederick II in southern Italy thus had two roots, a Saracen one and a Norman one.

We have already discussed the Arab or Saracen element in broad outline. Its potential as regards the development of a mechanistic way of thinking is closely linked with a particular characteristic of the Semitic peoples in the wider historical sense. This is their gift for logical, abstract thinking. The forces of mortality or death are at work in this type of

42

thinking, which was especially developed over thousands of years by the Jewish element. It is a logical, acute kind of thinking without images which can (unless it undergoes a transformation) be in danger of falling into a mechanistic mode. In the religious field this can lead to a form of abstract monotheism, while in social life it brings about a tendency to work towards unity in an abstract way that overlays the whole of life with a centralized network of concepts, rules and regulations which have been thought up for reasons of expediency and are applied in a mechanistic way that fails to reckon with the psychological element in human beings.[4]

The Norman element came with Robert Guiscard (the Astute), Duke of Apulia and Calabria (d.1085) and Roger II, (reigned 1130-1154) who, having conquered Sicily and southern Italy, created there a state that possessed its own army, consisting partly of mercenaries, and a fleet of considerable size. The necessary fiscal basis for this came from a tax system and a form of administration that 'bore the hallmark of the modern state'.[5] Describing the older state system developed by the Normans in Normandy, whence came the Norman conquest of southern Italy, Oswald Spengler had this to say:

'The Norman state with its cunning money-raising techniques was based entirely on the principle of plunder which made ingenious use of the feudal system. The barons had the task of exploiting the territory allotted to them and were obliged to pay a share to the duke. Wealth was the goal; it was bestowed on the daring by God. The modern fiscal system has its source in the practices of these sedentary pirates. From the treasury of Robert the Devil of Normandy (d.1035) come the words "cheque" (from the chequered pattern of the counting table), "account", "control", "receipt", "record", as well as the present-day name of the British treasury "the Exchequer". When the Normans conquered England in 1066 the barons exploited their Saxon kindred with equal vigour.'[6]

This unattractive though energetic and successful element took effect in southern Italy and led to a unique union with the Saracen, Islamic element there which resulted in the Sicilian, southern Italian state, won by the Hohenstaufens, becoming under Frederick II that 'first modern state' which Richard Schmidt described as follows:

'Judiciary and police were combined in the king's lawyers, justices and civil servants to the total exclusion of the feudal landlords; financial administration went to extremes of poll and land taxation combined with imperial monopolies, tariffs and dealings; feudal powers were kept in check by a large Saracen and German bodyguard; strict rules governing trade, the guilds, and study at the universities were applied with the rigour of

43

a police state; and the last remaining medieval constitutional barriers to the power of the king were finally abolished . . . It was the most energetic creation of a state in the Middle Ages . . . Its forms were destined for a great future, although it was to take another two centuries for its full effectiveness to be achieved.'[7]

The latter words refer to the Italian Renaissance states of the fifteenth century when the example of Frederick II's Sicilian, southern Italian state began to have such a strong after-effect. Thus Jakob Burckhardt began his great work on Renaissance culture in Italy with a description of Frederick II's southern Italian state as an example taken up by the autocratic rulers of the Italian principalities of the Renaissance:

'His childhood having been spent surrounded by treachery and danger, he had become accustomed at an early age to be entirely objective in his assessment and treatment of situations. He was the first modern human being to occupy a throne. Added to this was a close and intimate knowledge of the inner workings and administration of the Saracen states . . .Frederick's edicts, especially after 1231, were aimed at achieving absolute royal power, the complete destruction of the feudal state, and the transformation of the people into a weak-willed, unarmed, gullible mass. He centralized judiciary and administration to a degree hitherto unknown in the west, not by means of abolishing the feudal courts but by ensuring that the imperial courts appointed the judges. Election by the people was forbidden as a means of filling any post, on pain of destruction of the town or village in question and the degradation of its population to serfdom. Internal taxes were collected by means of barbarous torture, without which it must, however, be admitted, no Oriental can be parted from his money. Populations were reduced to an easily controlled mass of subjects who, for example, were obliged to obtain special permission to marry outside their borders, and who were most emphatically not permitted to attend university elsewhere, especially not in Guelph-dominated Bologna. The University of Naples enforced the first known obligatory programme of study, whereas in the Orient - in this, at least - people were left free to make their own decisions. Typically Mohammedan, on the other hand, was the way Frederick traded all over the Mediterranean, reserving salt, metals and other merchandise for himself while hindering trading by his subjects. The Fatimid caliphs had, initially at least, been tolerant with regard to the religions preferred by their subjects. Frederick, on the other hand, crowned his system of government by the persecution of heretics . . . His internal police as well as the core of his army consisted of . . . Saracens who were impervious to every plea and indifferent to excommunication from the Church . . .'[8]

It is very strange that the same Staufen Emperor Frederick II, with whom the imperial universalism of the Middle Ages came to an end, should, at a turning point in time, with his creation of a rationalistic state in southern Italy, have given the first powerful impetus to a development that was to lead to the complete overcoming of everything medieval in social life.

To this significant phenomenon a further important circumstance may be added. Within this Norman, Saracen state lay territories that have played an important role in the cultural and spiritual history of mankind. Pythagoras had worked in southern Italy, and Empedocles in Sicily. Later on, in the Middle Ages, as though in the shadowy lee of that great spiritual past, the darkest of forces took up their abode there. These territories had become the seat of opposition to the Holy Grail, opposition linked with the name of Klingsor, about which Rudolf Steiner spoke very seriously as the source of much harm. In this connection he mentioned the fact that in 1194 Sibyl, the wife of the last Norman king, had fled with her son William to the castle of Calatabellota in Sicily, in other words, to the place where the powers of Klingsor, enemy of the Holy Grail, held sway.[9] She was fleeing from the Hohenstaufen Emperor Henry VI, husband of the Norman princess Constance, daughter of Roger II and heir to the Norman kingdom in southern Italy. The son of Henry VI and his wife Constance was Frederick II, who was born in the same year of 1194.[10]

Another factor in the sinister goings-on around Klingsor mentioned by Rudolf Steiner are the strongly Arabic influences at work there,[11] and there is no doubt that we are concerned here with one of the strongest consequences of the impulse of 666.

This, then, was the region in which the Sicilian state of Frederick II came into being in the thirteenth century.

We have already mentioned that this state played an important part in connection with the rise of the Renaissance states of central and northern Italy in the fifteenth century, which in turn became the seed and starting-point for much that has come into being in more recent centuries as the European states have developed their own social history. Even in the thirteenth century, however, Frederick II's state in Sicily appears to have had a direct influence on Germany. It was one of the influences on the rulers of the rising German territorial states from which, in turn, the modern states of central Europe have emerged. Spangenberg named a number of German princes who rose to power and esteem in the new young states of the thirteenth century:

'Unmistakable absolutist tendencies appeared, even then. It is quite conceivable that the early appearance of the "first modern state" created by Friedrich II of Hohenstaufen in southern Italy gave an effective stimulus to the German territorial princes, especially as they, too, were anyway going in a similar direction of a centrally organized regime. There was a close contact between the princes and Frederick II, who several times ordered them to attend court or imperial gatherings in Italy, so the influence of his powerful personality is sure to have had some bearing on them, whether to a greater or a lesser extent.' Spangenberg also pointed out in this connection that the position of the court judge taken on board by the German principalities was a Sicilian institution: 'Sicily's example must have borne fruit. The principalities became states run by civil servants, while the Empire remained feudal.'[12]

With all this in mind regarding the influence of Arabic culture on central Europe, there appears to be a profound historical symbolism in the fact that woven into the hem of the coronation mantle of the later German emperors is the message that Arabs in Sicily made it in the 528th year of the Hegira in Palermo for the Norman king Roger II. Henry VI, husband of Constance, captured it together with the Norman crown jewels; and Frederick II seems to have included it among the treasures of the realm. The coronation shoes and sandals are of the same origin.[13]

The Republic of Venice was another place in medieval Italy where 'modern' elements of politics and the state emerged early. We have already mentioned that from here an Ahrimanic spirit entered into the Crusades, as illustrated, for example, in the way holy relics became the foundation for the creation of capital under the influence of Venetian commerce. We have also mentioned[14] that Rudolf Steiner described the doge, Enrico Dandolo, as an incarnation of the Ahrimanic spirit. He died in 1205.

The mechanistic element in the constitution and administration of the state was developed early in the aristocratic city republic of Venice. Diplomacy in the modern sense first came into being in Venice. Indeed, the Venetian state is seen as the greatest school of diplomacy, and for many centuries historians favoured the reports of Venetian diplomats as being particularly clear and sober accounts of European diplomatic and political relationships. The science of statistics also originated in Venice.

Venice was also the home of utterly unscrupulous and callous 'Machiavellian' politics. A famous aspect of this was the cabinet of poisons maintained by the Republic for the purpose of getting rid of irksome opponents.

In the fifth post-Atlantean era this mechanistic impulse proceeded to develop and finally engulfed social and political life. The mechanistic impulse of Arabian origin joined forces with the Roman idea of the state and the law, and this led to the rise of the modern mechanistic state.[15]

11. The Templars and Philip the Fair

Beginning one after the other and playing into one another in many different ways, three streams of esoteric Christianity flowed through the Middle Ages and on into more modern times: the stream of the Holy Grail, the stream of the Templars and the stream of the Rosicrucians. In the narrow sense the Grail stream had its temporal home in the early Middle Ages while that of the Templars began at the height of the Middle Ages. The Rosicrucian stream did not appear until the thirteenth century, reaching its culmination towards the end of the Middle Ages and flowing on into modern times. It was involved in sowing and cultivating in the proper way the seeds of the age of natural science.[1]

All three streams flowed from the deepest workings of the powers of good directly responsible for the progress of mankind, and each was opposed by other forces of a different kind. Genuine history is the outcome of the way these streams and anti-streams flowed side by side with and in opposition to one another, and it is important to take them into account in endeavouring to comprehend the dynamic of history.

The stream of the Holy Grail[2] was opposed by the anti-Grail stream linked to the figure of Klingsor and rooted in southern Italy and Sicily.

The esoteric Christian stream of the Templars faced the destructive wave of Ahrimanic, Mephistophelian forces who used Philip the Fair as their tool.

Rosicrucianism was opposed by powers whose aim it was to 'abolish' not only the spirit but also the soul.

Just as these streams of esoteric Christianity were intimately linked with one another because they derived their inspiration from the same source, so, for the same reason, were the streams that opposed them inextricably intertwined.

*

We shall here discuss the tragic drama of the Templars - a drama of universal historical significance - in more detail because it can throw much light on many aspects of spiritual, cultural and social evolution.

Rudolf Steiner gave a moving description of the nature of the Templar's Order. Arising in 1118 out of the impulse of the Crusades and providing an impressive accompaniment to them, the order dedicated itself entirely to the service of the Mystery of Golgotha. Its most important seat was located immediately adjacent to the place where once Solomon's Temple had stood. Genuine members of the Order were filled with a holy enthusiasm for the Mystery of Golgotha and its Bearer. The Order's initial aim was to bring the holy places of Palestine within the power of the European will, and it was for this that the Templars had to be prepared to make any sacrifice. Everyone knew that the blood of the Templars belonged to Christ Jesus. The white cloak with the blood-red cross is like a symbol of this.

Any wealth gained belonged to the Order as a whole, and not to individuals. All the riches they amassed as time went on were to be placed in the service of their spiritual work. As a result of the sacrifices they made in the service of regaining control over the Holy Sepulchre, and as a result of the enthusiasm with which their earthly deeds were imbued, many Templars came to participate in a Christian initiation. Through experiences and mysticism of the kind unfolded by the Knights of the Temple, objective spiritual substance was brought within the realm of the earth. The Mystery of Golgotha was comprehended and experienced at a higher level. As the Templars spread from Jerusalem to the countries of Europe, all this 'gave an impulse to their souls that was intended to lead to a degree of spiritualization of European life.'[3]

Endeavours of this kind are, however, necessarily prone to fall prey to strong Luciferic temptations, and with this was linked the terrible tragedy of the Templars. Mankind was not yet ready to take in the impulses in the way the Templars unfolded them with such immense strength. The spiritual world was to come to human beings in a different way, and not by means of a rapid, Luciferic path.

In contrast there came the other power, the Ahrimanic power that worked through Philip the Fair and brought about the terrible end of the Templars, beginning from the year 1312. A decisive part in this was played by Philip's lust for the gold and treasure that had been amassed by them.

So what was there about that gold and that treasure belonging not to the individual knights but to the Order as a whole and intended to be placed in the service of spiritual aims?

Over many decades the Templars had become a considerable economic power, a great European banking house with its centre at the *Temple* in Paris. All their settlements incorporated exchange banks which had originally been intended for the convenience of the crusaders, accepting their money and issuing bills of exchange to be redeemed at the more eastern branches. Later this service extended to any prince or private person wishing to take advantage of it. The Templars even granted loans. Their international financial transactions enabled them to remit dues from the French clergy to Rome despite the ban on these payments by the French king, Philip the Fair, because of his dispute with Boniface VIII. This is a good example of the contrast between the European, Christian, world-wide orientation of the Templars and the territorially restricted, nationalistic attitude and practice of the French king.

The Templars were so at home in the world of commerce and finance that popes, kings and numerous other princes chose their chamberlains and financial advisers from among their number. Philip the Fair himself employed numerous Templars as tax collectors for whole provinces.[4]

Taken in a wider context, what does all this mean?

Being in a position to determine the regulation of capital is, in a wider sense, eminently a function of the spiritual, cultural sphere when this sphere is seen as having a beneficent, fruitful influence on external, economic life. Conversely, to order the economic life so that it is in keeping with the spirit, to fill it with impulses that are beneficent for humanity in a Christian sense, is the chief task to be accomplished in this sphere. Such tasks can only be achieved if the overall, decisive handling of capital is conducted by those who, rather than serving the ordinary, egoistic requirements of individuals or groups, possess a higher, objective, selfless impetus arising out of their overall view of the greater goals of mankind. This is a function of the spiritual, cultural sphere, as described by Rudolf Steiner, quite apart from any historical perspectives, in his book *Towards Social Renewal.*[5]

On a grand scale the Templars endeavoured to achieve an administration of capital and conduct of commerce founded on just such impulses. The most powerful spiritual forces are needed to overcome the resistance of the material world which is nowhere stronger than in the field of commerce and money. Thus, despite all its understandable human frailty and imperfection, the Order of Knights that was most deeply imbued with the substance of the Christ-impulse can rightly be seen as the one to have been most suited to tackling such a task. The way the Templars set about administering money and capital manifests the same traits of universal, western Christianity that also provided the impetus for the Crusades. The fact that this endeavour, too, was premature, going beyond the capabilities of people at that time, is also understandable, as is, seen from this angle, the terrible, tragic end brought down on this whole effort by the dark powers of Ahriman.

The endeavour of the Templars must also be seen in the light of the 'mystery of gold'. Rudolf Steiner hinted,[6] for example in connection with the *Nibelungenlied*, that gold belongs entirely to the supersensible world and ought to have no application in the world of the senses. The *Nibelungenlied* tells us to leave gold in the supersensible realm where it belongs because in the sense-perceptible world it will only make mischief. Thus gold can be seen from two opposing sides. On the one hand there is the gold of wisdom that used to work in ancient impersonal, selfless ways in the leadership of peoples or kingdoms in oriental, Atlantean theocracies;[7] and on the other there is the evil magic, the curse of gold when it is seized by egoistic, human greed and misused to gain unrightful power. The Templars sought to administer their gold and their treasure in wise and selfless ways, putting it at the service of an incipient social order in which Christ would provide the enlivening and shaping principle. Philip the Fair, in his dark and egoistic lust for gold, captured this treasure by means of his will for power in a centralist state. He became one of the main inaugurators of the modern stream of materialism. Not until this darkness is overcome will three figures shine again out of higher worlds, pointing into the future: the three kings in Goethe's *Märchen*, led by the golden king who is a picture of a future kingdom governed by a free and selfless spirit.

In the wider context of the problems arising in history as a result of the east-west polarity and linking this with the current estrangement between east and west, Walter Johannes Stein aptly pointed out: 'It will be impossible to reach an understanding with the east until the west learns to administer gold in a selfless way. The Templars tried to set an example in this. From the east they brought powerful impulses of light to the West, endeavouring to unite eastern goodness with Western realism. Individually, each was poor and without means, but they administered vast riches in gold. Their Order functioned like a bank working selflessly . . . The Templars knew that in gold the might of the sun lies hidden and that this world-wide might of the sun longs to be extracted from the gold.'[8]

*

In every way Philip the Fair appears as the dark and inimical counterforce of the Templars, whom he was to destroy. Walter Kienast described him thus: 'He was anointed in Rheims at the age of only seventeen. Tall and strong, his pale face framed by long, curly hair, he came to be nicknamed "the Fair". Very much aware of his royal dignity, and reticent in the extreme in public, he had a cold, immobile presence, almost as though carved in stone, that stands out eerily against the background of the terrible events of his reign. Except toward his immediate family his nature revealed no sign of human kindness . . . '[9]

Philip the Fair is one of those historical figures who embody, as though in a focal point, many characteristics. Everything about Philip augurs the dawn of a new age. 'The biting wind of modern history blows through his very being,' said Leopold von Ranke, comparing him in particular with his penultimate predecessor on the French throne, Louis IX, Saint Louis: 'Saint Louis lived within the idea of Christianity, whereas in Philip the Fair the thought of crown and realm was paramount.'[10] (Instead of 'realm' it would be more accurate to use the word 'state' in this context.) In Saint Louis (reigned 1226-1270), Philip's grandfather, the genius of the Middle Ages did indeed achieve a culmination in the best human sense, as did also the genuine and good genius of the French nation. Saint Louis was the friend and exact contemporary of Thomas Aquinas. He founded the Sorbonne, that renowned seat of theological learning, and also participated in the two last Crusades.

Another great figure who stands out in sharp contrast to Philip the Fair is his contemporary, Dante (1265-1321), in whom the sweeping, universal world picture of the Middle Ages found a kind of splendid apotheosis. In *De monarchia*, which has been called the obituary of the declining Middle Ages, Dante described the demise of the Christian and universal medieval concept of emperorship.

The impulses at work in Philip the Fair were diametrically opposed to that concept. They were the impulses that were to make of western mankind a 'many-headed monster', to use Dante's phrase, by shattering the unity of the Middle Ages and replacing it with quite other structures (p.24) that led to the formation of the new Europe from the west. These impulses are those of the territorial, centralized state based on nationality.

In a remarkable way the decisive beginnings of this new age coincided with the culmination of papal power achieved under Boniface VIII, of which his famous bull *Unam Sanctam* (1302) is a classic expression. Once the universal papacy had triumphed over universal imperialism it fell prey to the nationalistic forces of the French monarchy.

The various stages of Philip's relentless campaign against Boniface VIII can be found in any history book and need not be described here. By convening an assembly of estates Philip succeeded in popularizing his cause and raising the animosity of the people towards Boniface. Even the majority of the French clergy took the king's side against the papal party. After various ups and downs Clement V, now entirely dependent on the French king, was forced to move his residence from Rome to Avignon, thus initiating the 'Babylonian exile' of the Church (1309-1377). This was the Pope of whom Philip made use in his campaign against the Templars.

It is noteworthy that in the proximity of Philip, who so effectively contributed to the destruction of medieval universalism, a project should have been initiated that appears to us to be remarkably 'modern'. It is a project that gives us a sense of the way certain ideas, all stemming from the same wider source of inspiration, were germinating then, although they only grew properly in external historical reality at a much later date. We shall go into this briefly, especially as it is relatively little known.

Pierre Dubois, royal advocate, adviser and supporter of Philip the Fair, has been called 'the first typical political pamphleteer of the Middle Ages'.[11] Around 1306 he wrote a treatise *De recuperatione Terrae Sanctae* (The Recovery of the Holy Land) in which he suggested that in place of the old-fashioned universal monarchy of the emperor, still supported by Dante, a new international league of states should be set up by a council which would be proposed by the king and convened by the pope. By uniting all Catholics, or at least all Roman Catholic princes, a league of peace was to be founded. Any disturber of the international peace was to be deported to Palestine, or, at least, sanctions were to be imposed on his cross-border trade. In order to maintain this state of peace in the long term a permanent international European court of arbitration was to be established.

Here we have the seed of the League of Nations proposed and indeed realized over 600 years later by Woodrow Wilson. Even the sanctions are already present in Dubois' treatise. The underlying links are, indeed, even wider and more profound. Dubois' treatise consisted of two parts. The first part, describing the league of states, was intended not only for the King of France but also for the King of England and all the other Christian princes, including the Pope. The second part, on the other hand, was for the eyes of Philip the Fair alone. It encapsulated Dubois' goal of world dominion by France in west and east alike. This two-part method is not exactly honest; and it is in the difference between the public proposal and the private goal that we can discern a deeper kinship between Dubois' project and its more famous successor in our time.

Surely it is profoundly significant that preparations to put a terrible end to the universal, Christian work of the Templars should emanate from the same quarter as the idea for a different kind of universality, unreal though it may have been, a universality that would have served the egoistic purposes of a single state. The latter is like a distorted image of the Templars' endeavours, born of Ahrimanic impulses.

In his internal politics Philip the Fair became one of the most energetic and systematic inaugurators of the modern state in the Middle Ages. 'He was the embodiment of the state and he made sure that its absolute rights were represented and enforced against every other power by the men he trusted . . . His modern outlook is also revealed by the way he recognized public opinion as a force that could be deployed in his service.'[12] He applied this knowledge with much success in his fight against the Templars, especially by making sure that Pierre Dubois' pamphlets served to sway public opinion in his favour.

Another description: 'Philip the Fair was a man without any conscience; he was immoral as a matter of principle. His whole life was filled with hunger for power and with plans to extend his own power by fair means or foul . . . Seen from the vantage point of history his policies created the preconditions for national kingdoms. This fact may make it easier to understand, from the viewpoint of national necessity, the despicable means and foul machinations with which he pursued his aims.' Both in its content and in its attitude this latter sentence makes us sense that Machiavelli is not far away. In the fifteenth and sixteenth centuries he led his life in accordance with similar attitudes.

A third historian: 'Philip IV inaugurated a phase of relentless policies carried out in the interests of France . . . His rule was virtually absolute. "He is king, pope and emperor in his country," wrote an Aragonese ambassador. The maxim *Princeps legibus solutus* (the prince is above the law) from the Digest of Justinian[13] was taken up in France under his rule. He reigned in accordance with advice from the *légistes*, those knights of Roman law. His goal was the utmost strengthening of royal power. He achieved it more than any other Capetian king either before or after him until Louis XI.'

Ranke wrote: 'The large number of decrees in which he united the juridical, legislative and executive powers is astonishing. He interfered in every aspect of life, bringing in concepts of royal power. An all-powerful office of government emerged from the *parlement* (the French supreme court of law) and any religious considerations waned. Chief concerns were the rights of majesty, taxes, chambers of taxation, the levying of taxes, the right of the crown to own all the silver and gold in the realm . . ., the independence of the secular power and its decrees even in ecclesiastical matters, assemblies of the estates and the towns, the natural freedom of all human beings and the emancipation of serfs. It is understandable that this monarch should have roused the disgust of Dante, the great poet of that time, to such an extent that he could not help bursting out in vociferous disapproval. Equally it is understandable that a new age should have hailed his reign as its dawn.'

Finally, a description by one further historian: 'The *légistes*, those professional lawyers versed in Roman law, usually from bourgeois backgrounds but now acting as ruling statesmen at the king's court, increasingly take up positions in the centralized offices as well as in the provincial administrations. Thus a new political spirit full of legalistic dodges and court procedures, full of fraud and unscrupulous brutality, now enters on the scene . . . The forces of centralization are strong enough to make an almost absolutist mode of government possible. Just as theoretically the concept of the state is developed in an acutely legalistic manner, so in practice does the monarchy develop new methods in the fields of law and financial supremacy.'

'Financial supremacy' may sound like a wonderful concept, but let us look at the human and moral qualities, the personal and individual background to Philip's efforts, especially in the financial field.

Rudolf Steiner described the significance of this background.[14] He showed how Philip's soul was filled with a kind of enthusiasm by the moral, or rather the immoral power of gold, so that in a one-sided way he was able to derive his inspiration through 'making the wisdom of gold materialistic'. Making its wisdom materialistic is the opposite of what the Templars sought to do with regard to gold. Steiner called Philip 'a highly gifted personality equipped with exceptional, indeed with the highest intelligence' who 'was accessible to this inspiration through gold as a result of the most acutely Ahrimanic wisdom'. 'Philip IV, the Fair, may be described as a genius of greed, a man whose every instinct urged him to value only what could be conceived of in terms of gold. He allowed none but himself any power over gold. Whatever power could be enforced by means of gold he wanted for himself. It became a whim of historic proportions.' One consequence was his ban on the export of gold and silver out of France, a ban contravened by the Templars, who sent considerable sums to Boniface VIII. Another consequence, said Rudolf Steiner, was

Philip's endeavour to keep all the gold and silver for himself while giving his subjects merely the appearances of value by means of debasing the coinage. The people rioted, even calling him 'the Forger King', and the Templars also resisted the way he tampered with the coinage. In the end Philip had to flee the peoples' anger and take refuge with the Templars whom he had charged with hiding his gold. To his astonishment they managed to quell the riot with ease; but he feared their moral power, for it was a power that he lacked.

Steiner then showed how a passion as intense as Philip's passion for gold, one stimulated in a materialistic way, generates strong urges for power in the soul as well as knowledge of an Ahrimanic kind. (He also pointed to an inner connection with the essence of the dark Mysteries of the Mexicans.) Thus Philip was initiated into the evil principle of gold and became a tool 'in the service of Mephistophelian, Ahrimanic powers' who then used him for the great blow they were about to strike against the Templars. He lusted above all for the gold and treasure of the Templars and longed to seize it. But although this was his chief motivation there were also other reasons why he disliked the Templars, for they were a hindrance in his efforts to seize absolute power, which was the goal of all his internal policies.[15] Frequently he had had to make treaties with the Order as though with a state that was his equal.[16]

With the help of Pope Clement V, who was entirely subservient to him, Philip succeeded in destroying the Templars. The methods of diabolical refinement he used, based on the darkest occult knowledge, have been described by Rudolf Steiner who also added a great deal more to our knowledge of those hideous events, the exoteric side of which is, of course, well-known, events which can be counted among the most abominable crimes in history. Fifty-four Templars were burnt at the stake in Paris, including, in the end, the grand master, Jacques de Molay (1314). The Order of the Templars was then suppressed by Clement V.

*

We can here only sketch the further effects of the proceedings against the Templars and their execution, reiterating in brief what Rudolf Steiner revealed on the basis of his deep spiritual knowledge.

Becoming ever more sharply distinct, two streams existed thenceforward in Europe's further history.

On the one hand there was the stream to which Philip's brutal treatment of the Templars had given tremendous occult, spiritual stimulus and incentive. This was the stream of materialism that gained an ever more stormy and insistent hold over European life. On the other hand there was the spiritual stream which the Templars had endeavoured to serve. In this stream lived the Christian, spiritual essence for which they had worked in their most solemn hours, and now it had seemingly vanished from the face of the earth. It had been received into the spiritual world where it continued to live in an esoteric form, inspiring human beings who were receptive to it. It was a stream that was as though held in check, preserved for the future. From it, as Rudolf Steiner pointed out, flowed such inspired writings as, for example, Goethe's Rosicrucian poem 'Die Geheimnisse', as well as his *Märchen* 'The Green Snake and the Beautiful Lily'.[17]

This brings us, as though guided from above by the spiritual stream that now flows on high, to the time of the late eighteenth century, the time of the French Revolution and of Goethe.

Before following this thread, however, let us look at another, more externally known circumstance which in its own way is equally remarkable and significant, and to which Walter Johannes Stein repeatedly referred.[18] This involved the fact that by an extraordinary chain of circumstances the Templars escaped extinction in Portugal, where they continued to exist as the Order of Christ. Henry the Navigator (1394-1460) was governor and administrator of this Order. He played a decisive part in encouraging the Portuguese nation to take up its great seafaring mission. 'Navigation as such', wrote Stein, 'as well as the urge to sail the great oceans worldwide, stem from the traditions of the Templars. It was they who inaugurated the age of discovery that laid the foundation for our modern economy, and this economy will not thrive if it does not take its cue from the moral impulses that were of holiest importance for those inaugurators of our modern age.'

This shows how the exoteric stream left by the Templars carried on their impulse in so far as this impulse was concerned with the external world and the handling of the economy on an overall, universal scale. Stein also mentioned that the Portuguese Knights of Christ set out eastwards in search of Prester John in order to join forces with him on the side of Christianity and against Arabism.

We thus see the inclination of the Templars continuing on externally in physical history in quite a direct way. However, it must be admitted, as Stein pointed out, that although the original intentions of the voyages of discovery may have been entirely admirable and pure they were soon clouded or even wiped out when 'the lust for gold became their sole motivation as a result of the voyages to Mexico and Peru'. The later Spanish *conquistadores*, welcomed in Mexico as white gods, lived out their lust for gold that was richly nourished by the gifts of the Mexicans and Peruvians.

Once again the external continuation of what the Templars had intended fell prey to the same dark counterforces that were, in a way, at home in Mexico and that had worked through Philip the Fair, the Ahrimanic initiate of gold. Stein's imaginative way of examining the matter reveals to us yet another repetition of the tragedy of the Templars. Again this took on materialistic forms not only in the atrocities committed by the Spaniards in Mexico and Peru, as well as in other parts of America, but also above and beyond these in the more far-reaching consequences that followed from importing American gold into Europe. This had a substantial influence on the rise of European capitalism with its accompanying attitude of mind. It is like another victory of Philip the Fair, as well as of the Mexican past, over the pure impulses of the Templars for which the time was not yet ripe.

Thus, strongly influenced by materialism and the force of evil inherent in it, the age of the consciousness soul appeared on the horizon. Later, at the end of the eighteenth century, it was to face a great crisis that would have necessitated the inauguration of an all-embracing renewal, and this is what the French Revolution was all about.

Rudolf Steiner pointed out that the French Revolution, however high its ideals, was coloured and given direction by the influence of that event in the early fourteenth century through which Ahriman-Mephistopheles, whose historical tool Philip the Fair had been, had become powerful enough to insinuate the materialistic impulse into European life. The shadows of this event lay ominously over the French Revolution and led to momentous errors that have still not been overcome. These errors consisted above all in the failure to recognize the threefold social ideal that strove for realization in the French Revolution. This ideal could only have been comprehended and realized, however, if there had been an understanding of the trinity in the human being. If this had been understood it would have been possible to grasp that liberty is meaningful only for the human soul, that equality must be applied to the spirit that lives in the human ego, and that the ideal of fraternity has validity when applied to the human body. Only in this way does the threefold ideal 'correspond with the inner meaning of the spiritual world'.[19] This spiritual understanding of the human trinity was lacking in the eighteenth century as a consequence of the power of the Ahrimanic, Mephistophelian stream, and so the French Revolution confused the three ideals, applying them solely to external, physical life. Nothing but social chaos could come of this.

These were the effects that flowed from the stream of materialism. The 'hidden parallel' (Rudolf Steiner) to this stream lived in the spiritual world, and from it came inspirations which certain individuals were capable of receiving and which threw light on the future spiritual and social aims of mankind. In this connection Steiner expressly mentioned Goethe's Rosicrucian poem 'Die Geheimnisse' as well as his *Märchen* in which appear the significant figures of the three kings who are profoundly related to the three genuine, properly-understood ideals.[20]

Closely related to Goethe's *Märchen* are Schiller's *Letters on the Aesthetic Education of Man*. Like the *Märchen* they emerged from concern about the French Revolution and its meaning. Also inspired by the French Revolution were the ideas Wilhelm von Humboldt expressed in his treatise on limiting the power of the state. Although, since he wrote this as a young man, it has certain shortcomings, it is in its more profound aspects also related to those other works, all of which show various shafts of light deriving from the same source of inspiration that goes back to the events of the tragedy of the Templars at the beginning of the fourteenth century.

Even in the external course of events in the French Revolution there was a strange reminder of the Templars' story.

For the final few months of his life Louis XVI was imprisoned with his family in the *Temple* in Paris, whence he was taken to his execution on 21 January 1793. *Le Temple* was the last remnant, consisting only of a tower, of the former house of the Templars' Order mentioned above in connection with Philip the Fair. Having imprisoned 140 knights there, he himself had moved into the *Temple* in order to be sure of guarding their treasure which he had appropriated for himself. He transformed the *Temple* into his palace.[21]

In his history of the Revolution the French historian Jules Michelet said that the national assembly had left it to the Paris commune to choose where Louis XVI should be held prisoner, and it was the commune who had chosen the *Temple*. 'This squat, solid, gloomy tower was the former treasure chamber of the Templars. For years it had been a solitary place abandoned to decay, a place under the spell of a strange historical destiny. Here, through the hand of Philip the Fair, the monarchy of the Middle Ages had broken the spirit of the Templars, and now, in Louis XVI, the monarchy itself was to be toppled.'[22]

Was Louis XVI's imprisonment in the *Temple* merely a remarkable 'coincidence', in which case it would be even more meaningful karmically?

Or was it arranged consciously, stage-managed to create a symbol of historical retribution?[23]

The latter seems more likely, according to Lamartine, who stated in his *Histoire des Girondins* that no guests had occupied the rooms of the *Temple* since the Templars had perished at the stake. In this case Louis XVI and his family would have been the first 'guests' to stay there for several hundred years. Something else that could lend force to this possibility is the fact that the Masonic lodges and their interconnections were to a great extent behind the events of the French Revolution, and the Freemasons traced their own origins back to the medieval Order of the Knights Templar. It would thus not be surprising if, from among their circle, the idea had emerged to wreak belated revenge on Louis XVI, successor to the king who had destroyed the Templars. Such revenge would be aimed at a hated 'tyrant' who was, in reality, no real tyrant at all although he most certainly had inherited the princely absolutism that Philip the Fair had so decisively helped to bring into the world and to which he had sacrificed the Order of the Templars. The idea of taking 'revenge' on Philip's successor for the fate of the Templars would not only have fallen on one who was essentially innocent, but it would in addition have been an act that was far more in keeping with Philip himself than in the spirit of the Knights Templar. The imprisonment of Louis XVI in the former treasure house of the Templars certainly appears to be a most potent symbol of the times.[24]

The French Revolution should have had the task of overcoming the absolutist development of the state and bringing about the kingdom of the 'three kings' of Goethe's *Märchen*. In this task it most certainly failed. In fact, far from overcoming the work of Philip the Fair, the Revolution perpetuated it to a great extent. All that fell was the human being at the head of that state.

We could spend a further chapter following up the even later effects Philip's spirit had on France in the times following the French Revolution and leading right up to the present day. We should have to consider such phenomena as the gold piled up in the strong-rooms of the Bank of France, or indeed French policies with regard to gold in the widest sense.[25] In doing so we would stumble across links and interconnections that are playing important roles even today, in the tragic events and aberrations of the twentieth century.

Our present age with all its struggles and contradictions also stands under the sign of those two streams that issued forth from the destruction of the Knights Templar. The purpose of concerning ourselves with the

59

Templars and Philip the Fair is, after all, to learn to stand rightly within our own time in the light of a deepened understanding of the history that has brought us here.

12. Templars, Hospitallers of St John, Teutonic Knights

These three religious orders of knighthood are typical of much of the best endeavour that sprang up in the Middle Ages. Like the Templars, the other two also came about as a result of the Crusades. Their founding in the Holy Land arose from the longing of western Christians to find spiritual light in the east - a deepening and renewal of Christianity. This was more strongly so in the case of the Hospitallers than in that of the Teutonic Order, which was not founded until the end of the twelfth century when the fervour of the Crusades was beginning to wane. Rudolf Steiner saw an inner connection of all three orders with the endeavours of Godfrey of Bouillon to found a Christian focus in Jerusalem to counter the might of Rome, endeavours, however, that came to nought at the time.[1]

All three orders had in common the wish to work under the sign of 'Cross and Sword', as monks and as knights. The sword was to be wielded in the service of the cross. Another way to view this double symbol is to say that the sword inflicts wounds and the cross heals them, thus symbolically uniting the double forces of Mars and Mercury, the two great influences that operate throughout the evolution of the Earth. The first half of this evolution proceeded under the influence of Mars whose task it was to carry both the earth and human beings down into the firm and solid world of form. In the second half the influence of Mercury is to come to the fore, gradually dissolving the solid hardness and leading earth and human beings onwards to a new spirituality. Mercury must heal the wounds that Mars first had to inflict.

This double impulse of warrior and healer was present in an inwardly spiritual and social sense in the Order of the Knights Templar.[2] It was more outward and familiar as seen in the Hospitallers, and it appeared as well in the Teutonic Order which also traced its origins back to the founding of a hospital, the Hospital of St Mary, in Acre in 1190 when epidemics were breaking out among the crusading armies. Seven years later this was transformed into the religious Order of Teutonic Knights.

Despite all their similarities the three orders also show marked differences. There are varieties of emphasis which reveal a threefold development when all three orders are seen in conjunction.

There is a degree of polarity between the two older orders, the Templars and the Hospitallers.

Of all the orders, the Templars had the strongest and deepest spiritual impulses, and their initiation was an initiation of the will. Especially because of this they also sought to grasp hold of the material world by entering into the economic life connected with finance and the administration of money. This is the sphere of human social life that is most opposed to the spiritual impulses of Christianity. The Templars endeavoured to administer gold in a selfless manner in the service of the spiritual aims of human evolution. They became the bankers of Europe. Their mission is obviously connected with the tasks of the west, so although their Order was founded in Palestine they worked especially strongly in the west. This is also why they fell victim to the Ahrimanic powers served by Philip the Fair. Even their remarkable afterglow was located in the furthest south-western corner of Europe, in Portugal, where, as the Order of Christ, they inaugurated the seafaring mission that was to bring about the era of discovery. This in turn led to the discovery of America and also to the tremendously active economic colonization carried out by Europe in later centuries.

The Hospitallers of St John represent the opposite pole. They were oriented especially towards the spiritual element of the east. Their patron was John the Baptist, which is reflected in their name. In their profounder aspect they tended more towards the work of the Holy Spirit, which is also the Healing Spirit encompassing therapeutic work. The Hospitallers of St John were above all the Order concerned with caring for the sick. Of all three orders it retained its emphasis longest in the east. After the loss of the Holy Land, where it had founded a large number of settlements, it remained for a further two hundred years in Cyprus and then in Rhodes (until 1523) where it was known as the Order of the Knights of Rhodes. From here, and subsequently from Malta, as the Sovereign and Military Order of the Knights of Malta, it 'endeavoured, by creating its own sovereign state, to cover the retreat of the western world before the encroaching Turks'.[3] In this sense the original impulse of the Crusades that had been directed towards the east and the Holy Land was kept alive longest by this Order. The tragic failure of the Crusades meant that in the end all that remained for the Hospitallers was the task of 'covering the retreat of the western world'.

There is also a contrast between the Templars and the Hospitallers in the ordinary chronological sense. Of all three orders the Templars perished soonest, at the beginning of the fourteenth century, while the Hospitallers continued longest in existence as an extensive political structure. They only finally succumbed, admittedly by then entirely degenerate and anachronistic, to the storms engendered by the French Revolution. Having existed as a kind of sovereign state until 1798, they were administered the final blow by Napoleon - as was so much else that had become outdated - when he conquered Malta.

The last grand master while the Order was still a territorial sovereign state was Ferdinand von Hompesch, who was both the first and the last German to attain this position (1797-1798). The sovereign state of the Order came to an end while he was in office. There is a spiritual secret attached to Hompesch, hinted at by Rudolf Steiner who connected him with the Count of Saint-Germain. Seen in this light it is possibly not quite right to regard him solely as the 'weak grand master' who, surrounded by intrigue, was unable to prevent the fall of Malta. Perhaps he should also be seen as a kind of liquidator of an institution that no longer possessed any justification for its existence, an institution whose disappearance from the historical stage was both necessary and desirable. Regarded in this way it would appear meaningful for Hompesch to have allowed or been forced to allow destiny to take its course with the fall of Malta.[4] When he left the island he took with him two relics, an arm of John the Baptist and a fragment of the true Cross. The Order was no more.

Nevertheless certain members of the Order now declared the Russian Tsar, Paul I, to be the grand master. He had for some time entertained a rather fanatical and enthusiastic admiration for the Order. It is as though emphasis was once more to be given to its eastern wing without, however, there being the slightest connection with its originally spiritual 'eastern' impulses. Paul I sought to give new content to the Order, making of it a Europe-wide bastion of the nobility that was to stand firm amid the angry, democratic seas of the French Revolution.[5] This endeavour ended with the assassination of Paul I in 1801.[6] It had been an endeavour in the spirit of the later 'Holy Alliance'. The Order stemming from the time of the Crusades was to have served as a means of resisting, with the forces of the past, the storm unleashed on the world by the French Revolution. This tendency, perhaps more than any other, can show us with hindsight how justified had been the actions of the last sovereign grand master, Ferdinand von Hompesch, who would have preferred, it seems, to allow the Order to come to a natural end.

This strange *post mortem* extension of the Hospitallers in Russia may perhaps be compared with the continuation of the Templars in Portugal, thus revealing yet another aspect of the east-west polarity which we believe to be discernible in the fundamental nature of these two orders.

*

The Order of Teutonic Knights, also known as the German Order of St Mary the Virgin, occupies something like a middle position between Templars and Hospitallers. It was the youngest of the three, having been founded towards the end of the twelfth century, and the only one whose name revealed a relationship to a particular nation. This fact alone indicates its central European nature and a mission lying in the midst between east and west.

In a sense the Teutonic Order was like a synthesis of the Templars and the Hospitallers in that its rule resembled that of the Templars in relation to its military aspect and that of the Hospitallers in relation to its task of caring for the sick. This is another sign of the 'middle' character of this Order. We should not fail to recognize, however, that from the beginning the intensity of spirituality in this Order was considerably weaker than that present as inner substance among, for example, the Templars. This is understandable, considering the late date of its inception; its early years coincided with the time when the culmination of the Crusades had already passed. There is a sense of the spirit that had hovered over the Hospitallers having shrunk to a more diminished and human level in the cult of the Virgin Mary practised, certainly with the greatest inward devotion, by the knights of this Order, who were also known as the Knights of Mary.

The diminishing of the esoteric Christian element in the Teutonic Order is surely connected with its particular nature and goals which were directed more towards the political aspect of the life of the state. It was especially drawn towards this middle element of the social organism, and this was in keeping with its central European character which bound it intimately to central European and German tasks relating to the administration of the law and the goals of the state. Typical of this is the figure of Hermann von Salza (1170-1239) who was high master from 1210 as well as being political adviser to Frederick II.

Under Hermann von Salza the Teutonic Order took up the mission that was to lead to its most enduring historical effects. In pursuing this mission it achieved in Prussia the establishment of an impressive state entity.

The Teutonic Order's urge to colonize and create new states is illustrated by a similar venture that took place considerably earlier than the opening up of Prussia. In 1211 it was invited by the King of Hungary to protect the Transylvanian borderland against the heathen Kumans in return for extensive rights of autonomy. Hermann von Salza sought to develop the Order's colony there into a full-blown state that was to receive its Christian and ecclesiastical *raison d'être* through its ability to expand right up to the borders of that heathen people as well as in its establishment as an outpost on the overland route to the Holy Land. This also shows that even in this early stage the Order was committed to the great German medieval 'drive to the east', which it sought to underpin by creating a state presence.[8]

Although this venture ended in failure, Hermann von Salza and the Order drew conclusions from it which served them well when the next similar opportunity arose. In 1225 or 1226 a Polish prince called for the Order's help against the heathen Prussians, and this was to lead to that momentous conquest of Prussia by the Teutonic Order followed by the founding of the Order's Prussian state.[9]

This north-eastern mission of the Teutonic Order can be seen to be inwardly connected with a development which Rudolf Steiner said was essential for the proper future evolution of humanity.[10] He spoke of a 'spiritual marriage' between central and eastern Europe, a concept that has implications regarding the correct transition from the fifth post-Atlantean era to the more spiritual sixth era. The Teutonic Knights took up their task at the transition from the fourth to the fifth era, just as the age of materialism was beginning to dawn. Although what they created bore within it the seeds of many later problems and burdens in the relationship between central and eastern Europe, it was nevertheless a kind of external counter-image of that 'spiritual marriage', taking the form of a well-organized and energetic state that became a kind of prototype for the later sovereign Prussian state.

The work of the Teutonic Order in the land of the heathen Prussians passed through three phases each representing a further withdrawal from its more spiritual beginnings. Its work began with entirely serious and well-meant intentions of Christianizing the heathen in keeping with the Christian calling of St Peter. Soon, however, much more emphasis came to be placed on the purely political considerations of power; this was the phase during which the Order's Prussian state was established. Finally, when the true idea and ideals of the Order had become utterly alienated, economic considerations came strongly to the fore. Thus an exemplary economy, a thoroughly materialistic flowering of Prussia, occurred in the fourteenth century under the auspices of the Order. Perhaps there is a deeper connection between this development of the Order in the fourteenth century and the fact that around the turn of the thirteenth to the fourteenth century (1291-1309) the seat of the high master was situated in Venice. This was the very time when Philip the Fair was preparing for his destruction of the Templars. In 1309 the seat of the high master was moved to the Marienburg in the Order's Prussian state.

The history of the Teutonic Order in Prussia thus embraced in sequence all three functions of social life. First came the religious and cultural aspect; this was followed by an emphasis on the state and its policies, after which economic development came to the fore. The main accent, however, was always on the aspect of the state and politics, for it was in this realm that the Order of Teutonic Knights was most talented.

Although rather one-sided in its praise, Erich Maschke's book *Der deutsche Ordensstaat* gives a good description of this aspect of the Order and traces in detail the inner connections between the Prussian state inaugurated by the Order and what later came to be termed 'Prussianism':

'A comparison of the rule of the Templars with that of the Teutonic Order immediately makes it obvious that in the latter the concept of official service is much more highly developed. Above and beyond the general Christian duties and monastic tasks its content is so concrete that it can be directly applied within the hierarchy and administration of the Order. In the chapter dealing with "the modesty of the official" it is stated that such an official "should regard himself more as the servant than as the master of the other". This is a very "Prussian" way of putting it. Emerging from the Christian, Benedictine tradition we have here the beginning of a concept of office and service that can without any difficulty be applied within the state, which is exactly what the Teutonic Order did. With this view of service it built up its Prussian state and created an attitude towards that state for which no better description can be found than the word "Prussian".

'Just as the vow of individual poverty made possible an incomparably greater common wealth, so did the monastic vow of obedience increase the military capacity of the Order . . . Renunciation of individual will meant the greatest possible increase of the common will. This creation of the common will was the necessary consequence of the internal structure of the Order . . . '

Maschke characterized the tasks of the Hospitallers and the Templars before continuing: 'From the moment it appeared on the historical scene the Teutonic Order was alone in giving the massed will of men and knights a decisive and fruitful direction: towards the state. In this Order the common will was not suffocated by the power politics of common egoism; it became will for the state.'

We cite these sentences without sharing the value judgements or preferences they reveal, for we do not consider the sphere of the state to be any more or any less valuable than, for example, the economic sphere. What matters is the spirit in which any particular task is tackled. There can just as easily be a common egoism of the state as one of economic policies, or any other.

Maschke also stressed the stability of Prussia as well as the clarity of its structure which was unknown in any other medieval German 'state'. 'That is why the Teutonic Order's Prussia, like the Norman state of Frederick II, appears to be so "modern", although it is, in fact, not modern at all. What happened was that the Order was able to apply as a structure for its state the concepts of office and service, as well as the whole administrative structure, which it had initially applied to lands in its possession that were not yet states. Once the Order had attained the characteristics of a sovereign landlord and begun to operate the rights that went with this, all it had to do was transfer the administrative apparatus built up for its possessions in the Holy Land and in the German and Italian bailiwicks to its new lands, now recognized as a state, and immediately the "administration of the state" was in place.'

The transition from a religious order of knighthood rooted in the Middle Ages to a more modern state is here clearly visible. It is a process of secularization which was taking place everywhere at the dawn of the fifth post-Atlantean era and during the early centuries of that era. What we have seen is one of the roots of the modern state, a specifically medieval root. Its forces poured into the Prussian-German state of more recent centuries.

There is also another phenomenon to be noted in this connection. Destiny placed Copernicus, an individual who achieved much that contributed to the modern image of the world, in one of the regions conquered by the Teutonic Knights in the east. He was born in 1473 in the town of Torun (Thorn) and spent the greater part of his life in the service of the Church in the bishopric of Ermland (Warmia), especially at Frauenburg, which by its very name betrays the fact that it was founded by the Teutonic Knights, the Knights of St Mary the Virgin. He died there and lies buried in the cathedral.

The heliocentric and abstractly mathematical modern image of the world initiated by Copernicus is deeply connected with the forces at work in modern times. In the social field these forces led to something that might very well be defined as 'social Copernicanism'. This is the centralized modern state administered in an abstract way from a political central point. It is 'political heliocentrism' with the sun, the prince, in the centre around whom everything turns. This system of social Copernicanism reached a culmination in Louis IV in the way he expressly appropriated for himself the qualities of the sun.

Such likenesses, surmised rather than outlined in clear concepts, gain a more inward significance and gravity when seen in conjunction with something Rudolf Steiner revealed in the course of his supersensible research. He stated that the world-wide historical effect of Copernicus' findings received their hue and direction from the fact that this individual had lived in the prenatal supersensible world especially under the influence of certain impulses in the sphere of Mars.[11] Much that contributed to the rise of materialism in modern times emanated from that source. Mars forces gave the impetus for the centralized state structures of recent times and made them what they have meanwhile become. Mars forces were at work in the warlike and military activities of the Teutonic Order and later in a strongly militaristic, well-organized Prussia bent on conquest.

Two-and-a-half centuries after Copernicus there appeared the 'Prussian philosopher' *par excellence*, Immanuel Kant, philosopher of the limits of knowledge and of the categorical imperative, philosopher of the Prussian ethos, and we see how closely he was bound up with his home in the former land of the Teutonic Knights where he was born, worked and died in Königsberg.

The Order of Teutonic Knights came to an end (although it continued to exist formally for several centuries) in 1525 when the high master Albrecht von Brandenburg-Ansbach, a Hohenzollern, converted to Protestantism and, on the advice of Luther, secularized his fief, transforming it into a duchy for himself and introducing Protestantism to the land as a whole. This was the real end of the Teutonic Order; its mission had been fulfilled. The history of the former state of the Teutonic Order continued during the seventeenth century in that of Ducal Prussia out of which, in the eighteenth century, emerged the Prussian State in the sense those words have come to mean today.

At the end of the fourteenth century Philip the Fair annihilated the Order of the Templars; the sovereign Order of the Hospitallers of St John existed in Malta until the end of the eighteenth century; and the Order of Teutonic Knights came to its real end during the first third

of the sixteenth century. Thus even in its duration it occupies the middle
position between the two older orders.[12]

13. Poverty, Chastity and Obedience

There is a further example of the transition from the fourth to the
fifth post-Atlantean era which shows the metamorphosis of the driving
forces, of ideas and ideals in the Greco-Latin era, into those of our own.

The three monastic vows of the Middle Ages, the vows of poverty,
chastity and obedience, depict an ideal towards which a person undergoing
spiritual and religious development can strive. They are a means by which
the soul can school itself. The phenomenon of Christian convents and
monasteries must be seen in the first instance as having to do with the
schooling and purifying of souls in a manner suited to that time.[1]

There is no need here to consider what can be achieved by a genuinely
voluntary renunciation of earthly wealth, earthly love and the assertion of
a personal, earthly will. Our concern is to discover what emerges from
these attitudes of soul in the transition from the fourth to the fifth post-
Atlantean era. We want to find out what strengths they prepare in the
individual soul at the stage of the intellectual or heart-mind soul, strengths
that can later re-emerge at the consciousness soul stage not only as individual
qualities of soul but also as social impulses and ideals.

Properly understood, the principle of poverty for the individual member
of a monastic or any other order, the renunciation of egoistic possession
of worldly goods, points to the economic sphere where certain ethical
values are to be evolved. The individual possesses nothing, but his community,
the Order, may and indeed must own whatever worldly goods the members
need either for their own life or in order to achieve their common goal.
The members of the community make use of these goods in a fraternal
fashion either for themselves or for the outside world, for instance as
alms for the poor. There is also a fraternal quality in the way pious
individuals make gifts large or small to the Order so that it may have
an economic base from which to strive for a life of higher goals in spirit
and soul. Society as a whole has a genuine spiritual interest in this.

Of course there is no denying that gifts and donations to the orders
and to the Church were often made from egoistic motives, especially that
of achieving salvation in the next world. This is connected with
the way one-sided concern for the welfare of the soul after death tends
to foster egoism.

Chastity as an attitude attained in inner freedom has to do with the individual's right relationship with the spiritual world. Thus it is a precondition for all knowledge. It is connected with the fundamental impulses of spiritual life.

Obedience as a way of renouncing any assertion of one's own egoistic will has to do with the hierarchical structure of the world. The human being must obey God, and the lower members of the hierarchies must obey the higher ones. In human society the various levels of higher and lower persons mirror the heavenly hierarchy; this applies to the ecclesiastical hierarchy as well as to the inner structure of a religious order. Its latest worldly reflection may be found in the hierarchies of the military and of the civil service. All those at a lower level obey those at a higher level; and within one level all are equal, as are all human beings before God. Laws and rights, or the rule of a religious brotherhood, emanate from the divine world order. They require obedience on the part of all members of the community, and it is for the individual to make obedience voluntary, divesting it of any element of constraint. All this belongs to the sphere of politics and rights in society as a whole.

Poverty, chastity and obedience thus prove to be a means by which individuals in the fourth post-Atlantean era could prepare for a true comprehension of fundamental social principles in the fifth. By living through poverty in the right way an understanding is developed for handling the world of material goods in the spirit of genuine fraternity. As the Templars showed, such poverty can go hand in hand with the greatest communal wealth if only this is used to promote the spiritual progress of mankind. An attitude of chastity leads to liberty and higher knowledge in the spiritual life of mankind. And by a schooling in obedience a sense is developed for the hierarchical structure of the world which leads to the experience of true human equality such as is at home in the sphere of rights. Obedience applies to the ego as a member of the hierarchy of man; chastity applies to the individual soul that wrestles its way to spiritual freedom; and poverty applies to the human being who seeks a Christ-filled relationship with the bodily sphere, the sphere of material goods.

Poverty, chastity and obedience are related to fraternity, liberty and equality in the same way as a human being looking up to authority in childhood and youth is related to a person who has achieved the self-determination of maturity. If souls had not striven and schooled themselves during the fourth post-Atlantean era as they fought for the ideals of that time there would be little hope of achieving today's ideals in the fifth post-Atlantean era.

Seen in the images of Goethe's tale about the green snake and the beautiful lily we might also say that poverty prepares souls to assist in bringing into being the future realm of the bronze king, chastity creates preconditions for the realm of the gold king, and obedience helps to build the future realm of the silver king.

There was also a fourth vow, but significantly this did not appear until much later than the other three. It applied in the sixteenth century to the Jesuit Order which was not founded until after the beginning of the fifth post-Atlantean era and was intended expressly to be a weapon of the Church against the Reformation. In addition to the three monastic vows, members of this order also had to take a fourth vow 'to dedicate their life to the service of Christ and the Popes, to perform military service under the banner of the cross, to serve only the Lord and the Roman Archpriest as His earthly deputy, so that whatever the current Pope and his successors command for the salvation of the soul and the spread of the faith, and to whatever land they may be sent, they must obey without delay or excuse in so far as they have the strength to do so . . .' The main content of this fourth vow of the Jesuits was unquestioning obedience to the Pope. The higher trinity of vows serving solely the inner schooling of the individual is expanded into an earthly foursome aimed at external goals and placed in the service of the worldly religious power of the Roman Church against the Reformation.

For the sake of completeness it should also be mentioned that both the Templars and the Teutonic Order took on a fourth obligation in addition to the three monastic vows: to do battle against non-believers. This, too, is a step towards earthly purposes and away from the three ascetic vows that were to serve the schooling of the soul.

The fourth vow that reveals the real aim of the Order mentioned relates to the other three in the way the fourth king in Goethe's tale, the mixed king made of gold, silver and bronze, relates to the other three kings. The fourth king in the story is also the youngest of the brothers. He, too, in his social aspect, represents the centralizing tendency of the fifth post-Atlantean era with its orientation towards power. This is the selfsame social structure in which the 'Roman' social forces continue to work in their own particular way.

14. Secularization

We have already touched on one of the themes that can help us to understand how today's social and cultural life gradually evolved. All that originally received its more inward impulses from the life of the spirit, from religion and the Church, has undergone a slow process of secularization. It gradually came to lead a life bereft of contact with these origins, thus flowing more and more into the secular culture of modern times.

The later destiny of the Templars is one example of this. We have mentioned that their Portuguese successor, the Order of Christ, began the search for Prester John in the east. This search, still motivated by religious considerations, provided an impetus for the seafaring mission of the Portuguese people, which in turn led to the age of discovery, followed by colonialism and maritime trading.

Another example is the work of the Teutonic Order in Prussia. Here again the original motivation was religious: defence against the heathen and later their conversion. The outcome was that well-administered, extraordinarily 'modern' state in Prussia in which even economic and commercial matters were to a certain extent controlled by the state. It became the archetype for the later efficiently-run state of Prussia that had such a significant role to play once the fifth post-Atlantean era had begun.

The Roman church itself, with its organization based on Roman law, its wide experience and genius for politics, indeed its administrative practices and whole official set-up, became more than any other body the archetype of the modern European state. The earthly ecclesiastical hierarchy, founded on the heavenly hierarchy of angels in the sense of Dionysius the Areopagite,[1] became in turn the prototype for the structure of a secular state. The process of secularization leads directly from the heavenly hierarchies, via the hierarchy of the Church, to the hierarchy of civil servants in a secular state.

It is not without significance, as Rudolf Steiner showed, that two of the leading men pointing the way to the modern state and modern politics in seventeenth-century France were the Cardinals Richelieu and Mazarin, who in their very persons symbolized the transition from spiritual to secular.

Steiner discussed the same phenomenon in more general terms as well: 'The configuration of the Catholic Church has played a far greater role in general civilization than people imagine. Monarchies, even Protestant ones, were Catholic as far as their structure was concerned. Everything

71

in the world revealing the influence of the Roman world and Latin abstraction belongs to the fourth post-Atlantean era which requires human beings to be organized along abstract lines based on some kind of hierarchy.'[2]

These structures of the fourth post-Atlantean era are then contrasted in Steiner's lecture with the future spirit of the fifth era which is to be cultivated by spiritual science. Instead of such rigid or abstract structures this will require human beings to behave towards one another in accordance with what he called 'ethical individualism' in his *Philosophy of Freedom.* This contrasts sharply with the characteristic tenor of the fourth era.[3] It should lead to a social structure that is more than a mere secularization of the way the Roman Church was organized.

During the course of the later Middle Ages an independent secular social structure came to be recognized as having validity beside that of the Church, whereas earlier on everything secular had been as though overshadowed by a vastly superior Church structure. Secular princes had been expected to bow down to the Church, conforming piously and humbly with its requirements. This still found expression in the art of Gothic cathedrals. The French art historian Emile Mâle[4] pointed out that emperors, kings and barons were always depicted in positions of great humility beside the Godhead and the saints. Usually they are seen kneeling at the feet of Jesus Christ, the Virgin Mary or the saints. This did not begin to change until the fourteenth century when royal pride increased, but by then the end of the Middle Ages was approaching. Saints and martyrs were more important for medieval historians than kings and secular rulers. It is also significant that in 1080 Gregory VII deposed Henry IV for the second time in the main on account of his overweening pride in setting himself up against God, pride having been the original cause of sin.

The fourteenth century brought a wholesale increase in secularization. As regards philosophy it was the century during which Nominalism vanquished Realism. This was the victory of a view that had lost any perception of the reality of the supersensible world as depicted in concepts formulated by human beings. For the Nominalists perceptible objects in the physical world were the only reality, while concepts became no more than 'names'. Herein lay the decisive victory of the attitude that valued only what the senses could perceive, an attitude that led increasingly to the materialistic view of more recent centuries. This brought about not only the secularization and externalization of everything connected with the Church but also the great increase in superstition, which gained ground rapidly, taking on ever more absurd forms. Superstition comes about when phenomena that are true spiritually are interpreted in material terms. Significantly, superstition only became excessively grotesque during the later part of the Middle Ages. It was then that the phenomenon of witchcraft showed its most terrible face. As the spiritual connection with the higher realms of the supersensible world faded, all that remained were links with its lower and most dubious regions. This is the true source of witchcraft.[5] Superstition brought about a tremendous exaggeration of evil so that the slightest cause gave rise to suspicions of witchcraft. At the same time the Church, growing ever more materialistic, became less and less capable of counteracting genuinely evil occult practices.

So far as this murky region of decadence and externalization of spiritual things is concerned, the process that gradually enabled people to take hold of the sense-perceptible world by recognizing its own intrinsic value, as well as its laws, must surely be regarded as having been one of purification and cleansing. It was especially beneficial for the secular social order, the 'earthly city'. Hence the importance of such energetic representatives of Nominalism as the Franciscan William of Occam (c.1280-1349), who became known as *Venerabilis inceptor*. Contradicting the official view of the Church at that time, this pioneer of the inductive method and of empiricism taught that kingly authority was an ordinance of God and not of the Pope. Pope and king were regarded by him as equal, and so he defended the right of both Philip the Fair and Ludwig of Bavaria to oppose the Pope. Similarly his contemporary, Marsilius of Padua, in his famous treatise *Defensor pacis* (1324), defended the sovereignty of the people and their chosen king against the claims of the Pope. He stood up for the 'overall power of the state. The state was responsible for the attainment of both of humanity's goals, the temporal one as well as the eternal one.'[6]

Surrounded by phenomena of this kind the twilight of the Middle Ages gradually turned into the dawn of more recent times, founded on secular attitudes and culminating in the victory of materialism. The new age brought with it fundamental changes in the sphere of social life.

15. From the Middle Ages to Modern Times

The final centuries of the Middle Ages were influenced by the forces of Mars whose task it is to lead human beings strongly into the earthly world of form. In sequential periods of approximately three-and-a-half centuries history comes under the influence of the various archangels who are connected with Sun, Moon and the five planets and who take it in turns to act as time spirit ruling over human evolution from the cosmos for periods of about 354 years.[1] These periods are distinct from the longer spans of the post-Atlantean cultural eras which are connected with the precession of the sun in the Zodiac and last for approximately 2160 years.[2] (In this sense the fourth post-Atlantean era lasted from 747 BC to AD 1413.)

These longer eras of history are thus subdivided and also overlaid by the shorter periods over which the archangels rule in turn. Since 1879 Michael, the archangel of the Sun, has been the ruler of our present age which was preceded by the age of Gabriel working in the forces of the Moon. That age lasted from 1525 to 1879 and was preceded by the period of the Mars archangel Samael whose rule began in the last third of the twelfth century and lasted until about 1525.[3] The first two thirds of that period lay within the fourth post-Atlantean era (until 1413) while its final third belonged to the fifth era. It thus spanned the transition from the fourth to the fifth post-Atlantean era, which took place during the first third of the fifteenth century. That Mars-Samael period can thus be regarded as a kind of bridge from the fourth to the fifth era.

The impulse of an age does not appear suddenly in all its strength. At first, while the previous age continues to echo on quite strongly, it is more like an underground stream slowly gathering its forces together. Thus the true character of the Samael age did not appear fully until its first third had run its course, at the end of the thirteenth century. The Mars impulse came to the surface with great intensity around the year 1300.

This fact throws light on a number of things, such as the inclination to lay the foundations of the modern state partly on a military and partly on a Roman, legal basis. Another such phenomenon were the Mongolian invasions led by Genghis Khan and his descendants, which began at the end of the twelfth and lasted for the whole of the thirteenth century. The Mongolians themselves have a strongly Mars-like character and their mighty campaigns formed the introduction to the age of Mars.

Walter Johannes Stein pointed to another aspect of the Mars age,[4] showing that it was formed by the counterpoint of courage and fear. On the side of courage he placed everything connected with the discoveries of the fifteenth and sixteenth centuries, such as the work of the Order of Christ in Portugal, and also the courageous efforts of reformers such as Huss and Luther, while on the side of fear he saw, for example, all that emanated from the Inquisition, and everything connected with witches and witchcraft trials.

Another characteristic event of the Mars period was surely

also the Hundred Years' War between France and England (1337-1453). The invention and increasing use of firearms from the fourteenth century onwards is also a case in point. These weapons contributed to the demise of chivalry and led to the beginning of new ways of waging war.

All these and many other events of the late Middle Ages were expressions of the dawn of the age of the consciousness soul that is to evolve during the course of the fifth post-Atlantean era. Many conflicting currents were at work because the impulses of the intellectual or heart-mind soul that had filled human beings for centuries were gradually fading while those of the consciousness soul had not yet properly begun. The old had grown rotten and weak while the new was only in its earliest beginnings, and the consequence was the chaos of the later Middle Ages.

In considering this age Rudolf Steiner described the obstacles put by Luciferic and Ahrimanic powers in the way of the good spirit guides of mankind, especially Michael.[5] In connection with the story of 'Der gute Gerhard' written by Rudolf von Ems in the first half of the thirteenth century, Steiner described Luciferic aberrations revealed in the way mankind at that time lived in a kind of twilight, unable as yet to depict the physical world in thoughts of a purely physical kind but unable any longer to experience the spiritual world in a suitable way either. The two worlds were confused with one another. Physical facts were seen in imaginations rather than in ways suited to the physical world, and at the same time the spiritual world was described as though it consisted of physical facts and not of other modes of existence.

In speaking of Ahrimanic obstacles preventing the proper development of the consciousness soul, Rudolf Steiner mentioned the Hundred Years' War between France and England, saying that there were hidden intentions at that time to 'blanket Europe with a generalized concept of what a state should be. This concept would have annihilated and extinguished the individuality of the different peoples.'[6] If these intentions had succeeded much of what subsequently came about during the following centuries as a result of the interplay between the different peoples would have been impossible, especially the role played by France in the cultural and spiritual life of mankind as a whole in recent times.

This threat hanging not only over France but also over England, and indeed the whole world, if England and France had become a single conglomerate instead of two distinct states, was successfully countered by the Maid of Orleans (1412-1431) working in the service of the powers of Michael. Steiner described her appearance and destiny as 'an event revealing particularly clearly the way spiritual elements flowed into earthly events' at that time of confusion through which the age of the consciousness soul was to have been prevented.[7] The deliverance of France by the Maid of Orleans secured the further development of the various individual peoples of Europe. It was a victory that benefited not only the victor but also the vanquished, and indeed the whole world, and this surely shows that it bears the stamp of Michael.

The forces of chaos and confusion reigning in those times may also be seen in the internal social life of the various countries. As personalities grew more distinct, the old unifying forces of community belonging to the age of the intellectual or heart-mind soul began to disappear, while there was still a lack of new social structures that could have established a new order. In relation to the German lands one historian described the situation as follows:

'More and more the social and political conflicts of the fourteenth century came to a head in a feeling of uncertainty with regard to life in general including trade and commerce, and also in a deplorable decadence. There was a general sense of living under untenable circumstances from which the only escape lay in the re-establishment of law and justice, legality and order. What was needed, so people felt, was a sovereign power, a proper ruler who would protect the weak, smooth over the strife between town and country, balance out social and political conflicts and generally protect life and commerce. Gradually it became obvious that freedom and commerce could not flourish while all and sundry pursued their own interests without let or hindrance, nor while each individual sought only his own advantage and remained his own master in every respect.'[8]

One aspect of the crisis is typified by what was meant by law. The Germanic or German law of the Middle Ages had been woven out of instinctive forces founded in human feelings and had blossomed at a time when the Germanic peoples had as yet no awareness of individuality as such. I have pointed out elsewhere[9] how this German sense for the meaning of law entered into a critical phase around the fifteenth century when a new kind of consciousness was beginning to dawn. There was a need to evolve a new, contemporary legal system that would do justice to the awakening human individuality and the changing needs of the times.

Another aspect of life in which the disintegration of old ways was leading to chaos, accompanied by the search for new solutions, was that of religion and the Church. 'What history refers to as the evils and abuses of religious life which were dealt with by the great reforming Councils

76

in the age when the consciousness soul was beginning its activity,' wrote Rudolf Steiner, 'were connected with the life of those human souls who, not yet feeling themselves to be within the consciousness soul, were, on the other hand, no longer able to find in the old intellectual or heart-mind soul a sufficient source of inner strength or certainty.'[10]

Everywhere the old was being shaken to its foundations while the search for the new proceeded, the search for a new attitude towards the world and towards life, the search for a new order.

*

Like many questions in world history, the question as to the nature of this new order arising out of a creative chaos cannot be answered simply by pointing to what actually came about. We also have to ask which possibilities for development existed. A distinction has to be drawn between what a number of very disparate spiritual beings wanted, intended or gave their support to, and what finally emerged.

At the threshold to the new age stands the great figure of cardinal Nicholas of Cusa (1401-1464) who demonstrates many of the tendencies and conditions of his age. Rudolf Steiner described him as 'a wonderfully brilliant star in the heavens of medieval cultural and spiritual life';[11] and he said elsewhere: 'This personality is like an outstanding monument of his time.'[12]

Remarks by Rudolf Steiner about Nicholas of Cusa lead straight to the centre of our question. In discussing the gulf between the old methods of thought and research, represented finally by the mystics of the thirteenth to seventeenth centuries, and modern natural science, Steiner stressed that today's way of 'reading in the book of nature' is not likely to lead to a mystical mood of soul. This, however, is not the only way of looking at nature. There exist spirits 'capable of developing from ancient mysticism a way of thinking that can also encompass modern knowledge, and such a one was Nicholas of Cusa.

'Such individuals show that present-day natural science would be capable of undergoing a mystical deepening. Nicholas of Cusa could have taken his way of thinking and applied it to modern science. *It would have been possible to lay aside the old ways of research and, while retaining the mystical mood, take on modern scientific research, had it existed at the time.*'[13]

There is a close correlation between people's way of looking at nature and the possibilities they have of structuring their society. The way of thought that led to materialistic, intellectualized natural science, a kind of thinking that cannot be combined with a 'mystical' mood of any kind, is only capable, in the social realm, of leading to structures that are mechanical and materialistic. A different life of the state and politics could only have come about if, from the beginning, natural science had been established in the spirit meant by Rudolf Steiner in the passage quoted, which would have been the spirit of the Rosicrucian stream together with that stream's attitude to natural science.[14]

In addition to his philosophical thought and scientific research, both of which were mystically profound, there was also another field in which Nicholas of Cusa was active, and that was the field of social and Church politics. His fundamental political and social goals were intimately linked and entirely in keeping with his spiritual endeavours.

Rudolf Steiner showed[10] that Nicholas of Cusa was, on the one hand, entirely in accord with the new direction of evolution brought about by the unfolding of the consciousness soul. This is obvious from the way he worked during the reforming Council of Basel and in general within the life of the Church when, instead of fighting the abuses and evils of the physical world with fanatical zeal, he 'tried to meet them with ordinary common sense, seeking to restore to the proper channel those things which had become diverted from it'. One example of this were his concrete ideas about the necessary reform of the Empire which even then was threatening to disintegrate. He suggested ways of strengthening the central powers in order to prevent this disintegration. On the other hand Steiner saw Nicholas 'having thoughts and ideas which revealed in a most radiant way the working of Michael's forces within them. Into the midst of his age he placed the tried and tested ideas which, in the epoch when Michael had still been ruler of the cosmic intelligence, had led human souls to unfold faculties enabling them to perceive the beings and intelligences of the cosmos. The "learned ignorance" of which he spoke was a perception over and above that which is directed to the outer world of the senses - a perception that leads human thinking beyond the intellectuality of ordinary knowledge into a region where, in ignorance or emptiness of knowledge, the spirit is taken hold of by a pure, inner experience of seership.'

The true stamp of the Michaelic and thus cosmopolitan spirit may also be found in Nicholas of Cusa's book *De pace seu concordantia fidei*, about peace and harmony among all faiths. Such peace and harmony can only be attained in that higher sphere which is also the sphere of 'learned ignorance' where the essential core of every religion, common to them all, comes to the fore while trivia fall away. This sphere is the setting

78

for a spiritual conversation conducted by representatives of the various peoples in the presence of the Logos. In the end this conversation 'in the heaven of good sense' leads to agreement among all religions on the basis of the kernel of truth present in each one, namely, worship of the One God.[15] The Michaelic influence is tangible in this work. It is clad in the language of older experiences in a manner, half imaginative and half conceptual, that is typical of the latter part of the Middle Ages. In the following centuries, however, the world at large showed no signs of taking up such impulses. Not peace and harmony but hate and strife held sway among religions as the various confessions became ever more politicized while religious wars, with all their dire consequences, also made sure that the very substance of Christianity dwindled rapidly on every side.

The same Michaelic characteristics also shone forth in Nicholas of Cusa's far-reaching social impulses.[16] Central here is the idea of concordance or harmony between things that are disparate, between Pope and Council, for example, or between Pope and Emperor, Emperor and princes, and so on. This idea represents a specific attitude of mind and is more important than Cusa's various other suggestions for the reform of Church and Empire.[17] What he had in mind was a sounding-together in the heart (*con-cordantia*) of things that are essentially different in such a way that they join together to create a higher totality. The Holy Trinity, the union of three different divine persons, was for him the spiritual archetype of this.

Cusa possessed an attitude of mind that could encompass opposites and unite them in a central spirit. The Michaelic stamp is obvious, and in future this will indeed bring about quite other concordances, for example in the life of society as a whole, in a way not yet possible at that time. His social impulse as expressed in his *De concordantia catholica* may be described as spiritual democracy. It was founded on a deep conviction that the human ego is capable within itself of finding what is right and thus uniting in genuine concordance with other egos treading the same path. This might be achieved, for example, by all the Church representatives attending a Council.

These ideas are utterly un-Roman. Their aim is not absolutism, either of the Pope within the Church or of kings or princes in secular society. In Cusa's sense a prince's power to rule is derived from the people; only the concordance of those who will be subject to another's rule can provide a proper basis for that rule. In contrast to the Roman principle that places the prince above the law, Cusa stated that no prince should consider himself above the law.[18] These thoughts and impulses are not directed to social or state-run 'Copernicanism' but to the free, harmonious working-together of individual human egos, or of various offices or other bodies of the social organism.

The very fact that the thoughts and impulses of Nicholas of Cusa are so Michaelic helps us to understand why they were not destined to take hold of the immediate future of the fifteenth and sixteenth centuries or even later ones. These centuries were dominated by forces that led not to concordance but to the territorial principality, a pattern that emerged in Germany from the ruins of the Empire in accordance with the egoistic wishes of the princes. These forces led to a form of state 'Copernicanism' that was not in keeping with the ideas of Nicholas of Cusa but in direct opposition to them. If human beings had been mature enough for his ideas, the whole evolution of recent history would have been fundamentally different. Thought and life would not have become so materialistic and mechanistic, and the downward trend would have plunged less deeply than it in fact did. In the social realm the counterpart would have developed of what Rudolf Steiner described in connection with Nicholas of Cusa regarding the natural sciences and the scientific attitude. Old, worn-out social structures would have been discarded while the spiritual attitude on which they had been founded would have been retained and taken forward into something new from which new social structures more fitting for the age would have been able to emerge.

However, history followed a different course which showed even in the biography of Cusa himself. He had borne within him the fundamental idea of concordance, including that of concordance between Pope, who should have been first among equals, and Council. Yet towards the end of the Council of Basel he went over to the side of Pope Eugenius IV, whose authority he championed henceforth. He must have concluded that there was no foundation for the concordance he so earnestly desired, while at the same time recognizing that the one-sided anti-papal radicalism of the majority of the Council at Basel would certainly fail to lead to any harmonious development. This latter he knew could only come about through inner transformation and not by means of external battles or other methods involving the humiliation of the Pope.

This may well have been the motivation behind Cusa's 'change of position'. It also conforms with Rudolf Steiner's discussion of Cusa and of this point in a wider context when he described him as a great churchman on the one hand and on the other as one of the greatest thinkers of all time. Steiner also saw Nicholas of Cusa as 'an individual who probably understood himself quite well but who in some ways poses considerable problems for later observers'.[19] He spoke about Cusa's genius for understanding what was really needed in the social situation of his time and he contrasted this with the social chaos prevalent in all spheres of society.

'He threw himself wholeheartedly behind whichever side he was on,' said Steiner. Thus, at the Council of Basel, he 'led the minority whose ultimate aim it was to maintain the absolute power of the papacy. The majority, consisting chiefly of western bishops and cardinals, was in favour . . . of a more democratic kind of ecclesiastical administration in which the Pope was to be the servant of the Councils. The outcome was a split in the Council as a result of which Cusa's party transferred it to the south while the others remained in Basel and set up an anti-Pope. Nicholas of Cusa remained a staunch defender of absolute papal power, and with sufficient sensitivity it is possible to imagine what perceptions might have driven him to this attitude. He must have seen that what the majority wanted could only have led to a more sublimated version of the chaos already prevailing. What he wanted was a firm hand that could organize things and bring about order. He wanted this firm hand, but he also hoped that its deeds would be based on insight. Later, after he had been sent to central Europe, he continued to defend the strengthening of the papal Church, and this made him an obvious candidate to become a cardinal of the Church . . .'

Thus we see how even Nicholas of Cusa, in whose soul there lived quite other, more profound impulses, could not help but take the side of those forces that were to lead more steeply downwards into materialism in which society, the Church and the state were all to fall under the abstract, centralized power of social 'Copernicanism'. Cusa's change of position, connected as it was with the spiritual weakness of the approaching age of materialism, is typical of what was to happen over the next few centuries.

*

In this discussion of the transition from the Middle Ages to modern times we must mention, at least in brief, the Rosicrucian movement. More than any others, the genuine Rosicrucians were concerned to collaborate with the progressive powers of human evolution in bringing about the new age of natural science. Rudolf Steiner often called the fifteenth century the century of Christian Rosenkreutz, and in his considerations of 14 December 1924 he turned to an appreciation of the Rosicrucians immediately after discussing Nicholas of Cusa. The two

81

had in common their connections with the powers of Michael. The Rosicrucians, in particular, saw a profound link between striving to bring about a natural science deepened by spiritual and moral forces while at the same time implementing social impulses that would renew human social life in a manner suited to the fifth post-Atlantean era.[20]

Nevertheless, the Rosicrucians failed in their endeavour at the beginning of the seventeenth century to bring about a healthy development of social life. This meant that the downward trend towards materialism would continue for a long time to come. It also meant that what Rudolf Steiner described as being characteristic of the Rosicrucian stream would be unable to work openly during the years before 1600. The Rosicrucians worked inwardly, seeking to prepare in their souls, aside from their ordinary professional lives, a place where they could collaborate in spirit with the Michael-being, cultivating the ground for it. Thus they helped prepare on earth the spirit work of Michael for a later age.[21] In their own time there was no possibility of working openly.

*

Among the spiritual factors leading to increasingly materialistic ways of thinking, a strong influence was exercised, especially in the fifteenth century, by the sphere of Mars on human souls during their sojourn among the planets in their life between death and a new birth. Rudolf Steiner spoke of a kind of decadence prevailing in the Mars sphere that caused these souls, progressing towards a new birth at that time, to absorb impulses there which on earth made them open only to whatever could be perceived by the senses on the physical plain. This led to a purely materialistic comprehension of the world. To these influences from the sphere of Mars Steiner attributed the inclination, brought by Copernicus from his pre-natal life in the spiritual world, to view the heavens no longer in the old spiritual manner but purely abstractly in a mathematical way that conceived of space in terms of geometry.[22] The result was the Copernican view of the universe that came to have such immense significance in modern times.

Analogous with this was the 'Copernicanism' applied to the state and to social life. The social organism became a calculable structure that could be organized along more or less mechanistic lines. As in the heliocentric heavens, the prince took the place of the sun around which everything revolved; he became the fount of all strength and the source of every grace.

There is thus a profound kinship between Copernican astronomy and the development, begun centuries earlier, of the absolutist monarchy in its various forms. In France the king occupied the political centre of the country as a whole while in Germany the territorial principalities evolved. These monarchies, in whatever form, represented the 'firm hand' that brought order to medieval chaos. External forces of organization imposed order because the young forces of the consciousness soul awakening in the western world were still too weak to do so from within. The order thus imposed was in no way in keeping with the impulses of the consciousness soul; indeed, it constituted a retreat in the face of the tasks that were arising out of those impulses. The absolutism that evolved was, in the end, nothing more than a return to the social structures of ancient Egypt and Babylon, although the consciousness of the time was now an entirely different one. Instead of creating a social order operating on the basis of the consciousness soul and counting on the freedom of individuals who were growing ever more conscious of themselves, while at the same time achieving a communal life that did justice to this necessary freedom, society took refuge in an autocratic, centralistic form of government that had achieved its highest perfection in the distant past. This form of government created order and harmony because a single individual wielded all the power; all the others were not only forced but actually desired to bow down to this power because they saw in that one individual the embodiment of God on earth, the tool of the harmonizing, ordering power of the sun.

The voice of the tempter speaking out of the past was heard all the more readily because the dawning fifth post-Atlantean era was indeed linked by many 'subterranean channels' to the third, the era of Egypt and Babylon. Much belonging to that earlier age was to be repeated as a kind of echo now, but such an echo should have constituted a metamorphosis and re-birth out of the consciousness soul.[23] This is where the ways part, the one that leads to rightful repetition and the one that is actually nothing more than a relapse into the past.

One of the strongest means leading to this old-new situation, in which the monarch was all-powerful and government was a matter of abstract calculation, was recourse to Roman law,[24] long since defunct, that had been the end-product of centuries in which the people of Rome had evolved during the fourth post-Atlantean era. In the years of the late Middle Ages, when the forces of death had taken hold of social life, a secret attraction may indeed have existed between that social life and Roman law mummified in Justinian's *Corpus juris civilis*. Here was a sure and uniform body of law compared with the insecure and fragmented local, native law, especially that of central Europe. Instead of building on native law in the way Nicholas of Cusa had suggested, instead of transforming old laws founded on instinct into new ones consciously conceived, people succumbed, especially in Germany, to the temptation of falling back on the law of the Romans that stood there in all its abstract, crystal clarity as if waiting to be taken over with ease.

Thus, in this realm too, there was evidently a lack of productive soul forces during the early centuries of the consciousness soul age. In consequence, the 'reception' of Roman law may be seen to parallel the general situation of the Renaissance when, at the dawn of the mechanistic, materialistic age, people harked back on a grand scale to the cultural impulses of ancient Greece and Rome. The 'reception' of Roman law was also connected in another way with the change of consciousness that took place in the transition from the fourth to the fifth post-Atlantean era, or from the Middle Ages to modern times. Roman law may indeed have appeared to fit in with a keener and more awake individual consciousness. In some ways it was of a similar nature,[25] but in a deeper sense it was the law of the intellectual soul and as such did not belong to the new age which had the task of creating everything anew out of the consciousness soul.[26]

The 'reception' of Roman law began in the realm of the state, for it favoured the establishment of hard and fast rules of government. It contained the important principle of the supremacy of the will of the ruler which even in Roman times had been a throwback to the era of Egypt and Babylon. Now, in the late Middle Ages, it was music to the ears of the German princes who were thus even more inclined to favour the 'reception' of Roman law since it strengthened their own position of power and prepared the ground for absolutism. Thus it became a technical aid in the reintroduction of forms of rulership belonging to the third post-Atlantean era that arose as a result of incipient individualism and intellectualism.

Rudolf Steiner stressed the fact that the phenomenon of the German principalities was closely linked to the intellectualism of the time.[27] Speaking about Goethe's *Götz von Berlichingen* he pointed to the protagonist as being a good example of the way the mood of the people was opposed to the Roman law that had found its way into German life.

'In *Götz von Berlichingen* . . . old powers from pre-intellectualistic times confront one another: the German Emperor of former times, who must certainly not be confused with what German Emperors later became, the noble knights, the peasants, all from pre-intellectual times not yet "sicklied o'er with the pale cast of thought" . . . The play takes up something which had indeed once existed in more recent times but which had had its real roots in the fourth post-Atlantean era. All this is confronted, in a character such as Weisslingen, by what was then coming into being, the age of intellectualism that was so intimately bound up with the phenomenon of the German princes and which led on to later situations in central Europe right up to today's catastrophe.

'We see how in *Götz von Berlichingen* Goethe storms against these princes, how he looks back to times when intellectualism did not yet exist and how he takes up the cause of the old against what has come about in its place in central Europe . . .' Steiner went on to point out how Goethe turned, in a sense, to 'what had once been, although he cannot have wished to see it reappear in its old form. What he wanted was for things to take a different course. It is most interesting to observe this mood in Goethe and to see how he rebels against all that has come to take the place of Götz's world.'[28]

In Germany, and indeed throughout Europe, the absolutist principality was preceded by a system of 'government by estates' which was markedly dualistic, in which prince and estates together formed a *territorium*, which later became the state. (p.41) On the one hand the estates initially held the self-interest and despotism of the prince in check although on the other they represented a certain amount of internal fragmentation. Gradually the power of the prince grew stronger than that of the estates. Increasingly he became the man at the centre around whom those bodies formed which later became state institutions, namely, the judiciary and the administration.

The central authority was the council which became especially important for the formation of the state because the individual councillors, especially those with a legal training, were the first to harbour a modern awareness of what a state might be. They understood this better than did the prince or king;[29] and they were the true bearers of the Roman attitude to the state. Since it was the prince or king, together with his institutions, who brought about the unification of the state, he was also the bearer of this whole development, and this meant that absolutism was inherent in it from the beginning. Seen from another angle this can be regarded as 'the unavoidable reaction to the almost anarchic fragmentation of the preceding era.'[30] The energetic will of prince or king imposed order, in the sense of abstract unity, from outside since people were not yet mature enough to cope with a freer structure or with governing the various sections of life themselves within a more organic situation.

85

France is the 'classic' example of a modern centralized state. The tendency towards the 'logically' constructed state was here compounded because it was met by the natural French inclination to live in the intellectual soul. Thus a great capacity for logic has held sway throughout French history. As a result the Germanic elements that always tended towards differentiation, or 'feudalism', were increasingly driven back while Romanism with its central monarch came increasingly to the fore. Despite many setbacks, this development progressed with an astonishing consistency over the centuries. As we have seen, Philip the Fair was one of its important bearers. It had existed before his time but he gave it a decisive new impetus.

Not long after the reign of Philip the Fair came over a century of war between France and England with all its turbulence. Under Charles VII it ended in victory for France after the saving intervention of the Maid of Orleans. Charles' immediate successor, Louis XI (reigned 1461-1483), continued to elaborate the centralized state. For France and the French state this King represents the step across the threshold between the Middle Ages and modern times. His was an extraordinary figure.

'There can rarely have been a person in history,' wrote a German historian, 'whose character was so unlikeable yet whose significance was so great. Mean, bigoted, cunning, cruel, without dignity or courage, this King managed, with intelligence and ruthlessness, and by means of unscrupulous yet purposeful political manoeuvres, to remove every obstacle that stood in the way of his own absolute supremacy as well as the centralization of France. A terrible enemy to his enemies, he understood how to promote the welfare of his people and carry his state successfully over into modern times . . . He protected trade and industry, merchants and craftspeople; he made sure his subjects enjoyed the necessary freedoms, and despite strict political centralization allowed the provinces to retain their individual character. He was superstitiously pious yet strongly in favour of art and science. He opened the doors of France to the newly invented craft of printing and in 1453 welcomed the scholars fleeing from Constantinople before the Turks. He was a true Renaissance ruler who embodied the modern utilitarian politician, the ideal of the *principe*, long before Machiavelli had written his book.'[31]

A French historian wrote in similar vein: 'Of all the Valois kings,[32] Louis XI achieved the most for the unity of France and for the future of the monarchy. His reign accomplished the step from the Middle Ages to modern times . . . As regards domestic politics he succeeded in making the authority of the monarch felt by all and sundry. He was despotic by temperament and thus desired to be at the centre of everything. It has been said of him that all his councillors were united inside his head. His confidants were, on the whole, people of very bad repute who functioned as agents and spies . . . Mean and evil-minded though he may have been, the greatness of his work remains unsullied. Louis XI inherited from his father a country still deeply immersed in the Middle Ages and suffering terribly from the after-effects of the long war with England. When he died (on 31 August 1483) he bequeathed to his son, Charles VIII, a peaceful land no longer threatened by any aristocratic revolt, a great power in the new Europe, a France ripe for the absolutism of the future.'[33]

It is without doubt meaningful to consider what kind of human, moral qualities contributed in the main to the build-up of the modern, mechanistic state. Philip the Fair was one example and Louis XI another. A third would be the Renaissance politician, the type of prince who existed in Italy and provided the reality underlying the 'idealized' image of Machiavelli's *principe*.[34]

Thus was the new state prepared during the later Middle Ages. In a single structure it combined, firstly, the centralized power of the absolute ruler, secondly, Roman law and Roman concepts of state and, thirdly, the mechanistic trend of modern times. This structure then joined forces with the modern nationalistic impulse emerging from the west and so the western European nation state came into being. Gradually the system of European nation states was born. In the way they existed either with or against one another they replaced the medieval universalism that had been founded on Christian impulses.

In more recent centuries the power of things that are dying has become increasingly obvious as inborn human creativity has gradually declined. The world is growing ever more superficial.

Yet it is in confrontation with what is dying that the consciousness soul awakens. The increasing mechanization of the external world throws human beings back upon their own inner resources. Only in the depths of their own being can they find the principle of life that will one day work its way outwards again from within towards the world.

THE MONGOLIAN PEOPLES

Up to this point we have been discussing what might be termed the normal progress of medieval western humanity. In the thirteenth century that world was mightily threatened by a tidal wave from the east, an invasion by the peoples of Mongolia whose very nature was totally foreign and inimical to the culture of the west. Although the direct threat posed by Genghis Khan and his successors was averted as though by a miracle - apart from some transitory incursions - in another sense it exists still and seems to be subject to some far-reaching rhythm in world history.

The antagonisms in question arose from the oldest and most hidden contrasts in human existence. These reach back many thousands of years before the Christian era and point even further back to the time of ancient Atlantis. The Mongolian and the Mongolian-Turanian peoples bore within them elements that stemmed from the fourth and the seventh 'sub-race' of Atlantis respectively, namely the primeval Turanians and the later Atlantean Mongolians who resembled them in essence and who may indeed have been their physical descendants.[1]

The time of the primeval Turanians was that of the fourth Atlantean sub-race. It was in their time and on their soil that the great Atlantean disasters occurred which were the consequence of a decadence that consisted mainly in the misuse of magical powers, especially those involving the forces of life and of reproduction for egoistic purposes of power. This misuse also involved a betrayal of the secrets of the Mysteries.[2] Because human beings were then still so bound up with the processes of nature, the mischief unfolding among the primeval Turanians led to the natural catastrophes which over many thousands of years brought about the destruction of Atlantis. After this the principle of progress and further development in post-Atlantean times was nurtured by the fifth and also by the sixth Atlantean sub-race. From these stemmed the peoples who became the bearers of progress in post-Atlantean times, especially as far as the development of thinking and of the gradually-evolving freedom of mankind was concerned. Finally, the seventh sub-race, the Atlantean Mongolians, represented a kind of relapse into earlier Atlantean existence harking back to the primeval Turanians. In consequence much of the ancient Atlantean human nature lived on in the Turanian and Mongolian peoples, especially in eastern and central Asia.[3]

After the catastrophe of Atlantis, the enmity of the Turanian character towards post-Atlantean evolutionary progress appeared again in the ancient

Persian era as the counter-force to Zoroastrianism which amounted on a world scale to the opposition between Iran and Turan. Rudolf Steiner discussed this in depth in his lectures on the Gospel of Matthew. As well as a 'southern stream' involving mainly the cultures of India, he described a 'northern stream' comprising the Iranian peoples and others related to them. Their chief characteristic was one of tremendously active energy, a will to transform what had come down into external nature from the divine world. These human beings felt called upon to lead all this back once more to the gods.

Another strand in this stream consisted of the peoples living where Siberia now is, bordering on present-day Russia and even reaching right into Europe. These peoples had to a high degree retained the old clairvoyance which enabled them to look into the spiritual world. It had, however, become decadent, thus giving them certain characteristics. 'Such people have the urge to cultivate only that part of nature which affords them whatever they need for life; with as little effort as possible they snatch this away from the natural world.' Since they could see them, these people knew that there were spiritual beings living in nature. They knew them so well that they demanded to be maintained, without having to do much work themselves, by those beings who had, after all, brought them into this existence in the first place. Such was the mood and attitude of these decadent people with their astral clairvoyance.

In the ancient Persian era all these peoples were nomads roaming from place to place with their herds. They had no fixed abode and no particular attachment to any locality. Instead of taking special care of what the earth offered them they were quite ready to destroy whatever they saw around them if they needed any of it to support their own lives. Thus, as Rudolf Steiner said, arose the great contrast between these peoples of Turan and those of Iran. It was one of the most important aspects of post-Atlantean evolution and was the consequence of differing soul developments.

'In the north, in the direction of Siberia, was Turan, that mixture of peoples highly gifted with an inherited lower form of astral clairvoyance. Living in the spiritual world in the way they did, they had no inclination to found an external culture. Being rather passive by nature, and often having, even as their priests, magicians of a low calibre, they preferred as their culture a low kind of magic, or indeed black magic in some instances. To the south of these peoples lay Iran, where very early on the urge arose to engage the human spirit in transforming whatever the sense-perceptible world had to offer so that external cultures might emerge. Herein lies the great contrast between Iran and Turan.'[4]

90

The myth of King Jemshid points to the mission of the Iranians. Jemshid led his people to Iran from the north. From Ahura Mazda he received a golden dagger with which he was to fulfil his mission on earth. This dagger represents the human being's striving for wisdom by means of his external capacities. It served as a plough with which the land was turned into arable fields.[5] The Iranians became farmers and the great contrast between Iran and Turan is that between farmer and nomad. The Iranians felt themselves to be the companions of Ahura Mazda, the Sun God, whom they served by actively transforming the earth. In doing this they met with resistance from dark Ahriman with whom they connected the lazy, thieving Turanian nomads. Ahura Mazda, or Ormuzd, was the great Sun Spirit whose descent to earth was prophesied to the ancient Persians by Zarathustra.

Zarathustra's powerful royal protector was Gushtasp (Hystaspes in Greek). Inevitably the inspirations and intuitions brought to the people by Zarathustra and Gushtasp clashed with the ideas of the Turanians in the north. The resulting war between Gushtasp and the Turanian king was one of the greatest of all time and lasted for centuries.[6]

Rudolf Steiner also mentioned another aspect of this great contrast. When human beings leave nature to itself, as nomads do, it degenerates and grows wild. Thus the wolf is a creature that has become what it is through a process of decadence. Human beings, however, can use their own good qualities and spiritual capacities to tame the wolf, giving it some of their own characteristics. The wild wolf is transformed into the tame dog. Through their connection with the good universal powers of Ahura Mazda the ancestors of the ancient Persians were able to domesticate the animals and thus work against degeneration in nature.[7]

Domestic animals appear as the deed of the ancient Iranians while the wild wolf symbolizes the Turanians. It is like a picture of their whole soul life. In a deeper sense the wolf Fenrir of Nordic, Germanic mythology also represents old, decadent clairvoyance that has survived from ancient Atlantean times as a soul aspect immersed in the wild forces of the blood. Many centuries later, the ancestors of Genghis Khan traced their origin proudly to the 'grey she-wolf' so greatly revered by the Mongolian peoples.[8,9]

During the second post-Atlantean era Zarathustra prophesied the descent to earth of the sublime Sun God. From spiritual science we learn the profound fact that at the great turning-point of all time, when the Sun God was about to appear on earth as the Christ, this same Zarathustra was reincarnated in the Jesus of the Matthew Gospel. Once again the

Matthew Gospel tells of the dark counter-force now emerging in the figure of Herod who ordered the slaughter of the innocents at Bethlehem. This act of darkest magic[10] sought to slay the Jesus child of the Matthew Gospel, in other words the individuality of Zarathustra, in order to prevent the Mystery of Golgotha from taking place.

*

In the fourth century AD the Huns appeared from the depths of Asia and stormed across Europe. The name of Attila, their later king, harks back to Atlantis, and they did indeed emerge from among those Turanian-Mongolian races whose ancestors had lived during the final decadence of Atlantean times. Rudolf Steiner had the following to say about them:

'In all their customs and habits the Huns were entirely foreign to the peoples of Europe, so that they appeared to them as something utterly strange. They formed a compact unit and their devoted submission to Attila, whom they virtually deified, made them appear irresistibly terrible . . .'[11]

In its very wording this description characterizes the Atlantean nature of the Huns when it speaks of their forming a 'compact unit' in which there was as yet no knowledge of human individuality, and of the 'virtual deification' of Attila, which reflects the relationship between the Atlantean peoples and their super-human leaders and kings. Because of this they were felt to be irresistibly terrible and awe-inspiring by the peoples of the west who were the bearers of post-Atlantean cultures. The furthest advanced amongst these had reached the stage of the intellectual soul, while the Germanic tribes already bore within them the seeds of the consciousness soul in preparation for the fifth post-Atlantean era. These peoples sensed instinctively that the Huns brought with them a radical negation of all they stood for, something that threatened them with destruction.

The feelings of fear and terror aroused among the European population by the retarded soul elements of the Mongolians were also discussed by Rudolf Steiner in another connection. He described the astral bodies of these retarded races as being filled with 'substances released by decomposing astrality', substances that flourished particularly well in the fear and terror awakened in the Germanic tribes. As a result of this, European astral bodies became as though infected, 'and this infection re-emerged in later generations in the physical bodies not of individuals but of whole peoples. This is what leprosy was . . . that terrible affliction which wrought such havoc during the Middle Ages.'[12]

A similar, though different, description may be found in another lecture.[13] Here Steiner described the whole of Europe and Asia Minor as being still filled with demonic beings. These, he said, were the products of the decomposing spiritual forces of inferior racial elements that had played a part in the moral decline of Atlantis. Coming over from Atlantis, they had established themselves in Europe and Asia Minor but had then gradually died out and been replaced by better elements.[14] These 'demons of decomposition' living in the spiritual atmosphere of those countries had existed for a long time and were, much later, still infiltrating the feelings and sensations of human beings there. 'Thus, when large masses of people later came over from Asia at the time of the great migrations, including Attila with his hordes, filling the peoples of Europe with fear and dread, this fear and dread made them susceptible to the demonic beings still present there from earlier times. Gradually, as a consequence of the fear and dread, these demonic beings brought about the epidemic of the Middle Ages, which was leprosy . . . '

These two versions are not mutually exclusive. The 'substances of decomposition' may in part have emanated from the Huns themselves, while also originating in the other manner described. In both cases their source lay in the decadent elements of Atlantean races working on in post-Atlantean times.

History has recorded that the Huns met their first defeat in 451 in Gaul at the battle of the Catalaunian plains. Their final, decisive defeat came in 452 in Italy 'when Leo the Great, Bishop of Rome, stepped out to meet Attila and persuaded him to retreat. Leo knew what power it was that Attila exercised over his people. But Attila, with all his power, did not comprehend the power of Christianity that came out to meet him, so he submitted.'[15]

In another lecture, Rudolf Steiner pointed out that Attila appeared in Europe and only drew to a halt when he came up against Christianity because this was greater than anything possessed by the Huns. The Huns served their gods in a manner stemming from Atlantean culture, a manner more splendid than anything they had met on their way. Only Christianity itself impressed them.[16]

Raphael, steeped as he was in the healing power of Christianity, painted this scene in a mural in the Vatican. Against the backdrop of the city of Rome, Pope Leo with the triple crown on his head, accompanied by two cardinals, approaches Attila and his wild hordes on their horses with the sign of the cross. Leo and his company are utterly calm and above them are seen the figures of the apostle princes Peter and Paul with swords in their hands. Glancing upwards, Attila sees them and draws back. The Christian spirit of the west has brought him to a halt.

Attila died during the following year and his kingdom disintegrated. The threat posed by the Huns, this particular Mongolian threat, had been overcome.

There is also an interesting and valuable lecture by Maria von Nagy about Attila and the Huns.[17] She pointed out that the first campaigns of the Huns provided the trigger for the great migrations. The purpose of these migrations was to work against the Ahrimanic powers who were aiming to bring about a general mechanization of life by means of the Roman Empire (p.7). Attila, a high initiate in the Atlantean Mysteries, knew of the task of the great migrations and wanted to serve it, as the 'Scourge of God'. At the time when he began his victorious campaigns he was already known to the majority of peoples in the region of Germany; they recognized his mission. As well as Huns there were many Germanic peoples in his armies. 'His impulse joined forces with that of the Germanic peoples in the service of humanity's future against the power of Rome.' In the battle of the Catalaunian plains the Huns were much weakened, but the Roman army of Aetius was annihilated. When Attila then approached Italy, where Pope Leo forced him to turn back, his task had already been accomplished since he had destroyed the Roman army. He was able to withdraw when he, the initiate of ancient Atlantis, recognized in Leo the representative of the new initiation. His life, and with it his realm, came to an end soon after his return - an outcome known to him and his peoples from the beginning.

Von Nagy also had something significant to say about Attila's burial: 'He was laid in a tripartite coffin made of gold, silver and iron. The river Tisza was diverted from its bed. The coffin, together with those who wanted or were forced to die with him, were buried there and the waters then returned to their course.'

The tripartite coffin of gold, silver and iron reminds us of the old monotheistic theocracies which unified the life of spirit and culture, the life of rights, and the economic life, or - it could be said - the kingdoms of the 'golden', the 'silver' and the 'bronze' king; and Attila's watery grave could be likened to the great grave of Atlantis lying beneath the surging waves of the Flood.

Another aspect revealed in Raphael's mural of Leo's encounter with Attila outside the walls of Rome is the healing, Mercurial power of Christianity which alone is capable, in a deeper sense, of overcoming the Mongolian race of Mars. The powers of Mercury must take over from those of Mars, transforming and healing them. This dynamic is inherent in the overall evolution of humanity.

Several hundred years after Attila, in the eighth century, the Avars, Mongolian-Turanian kinsmen or descendants of the Huns, invaded Bavaria. They were vanquished by Charlemagne. From 900 onwards nomadic Hungarian horsemen threatened central and western Europe. They were conquered in 955 by the German King Otto I in the famous battle by the river Lech. Borne ahead of the German army went the banner depicting the warrior archangel Michael who was at that time the leading spirit of the German peoples. Once again we see in symbolic form how the spiritual might of western Christianity, standing at that time for human evolution as a whole, was the only force able to overcome the Turanian-Mongolian nature of Atlantean times. Michael, for his part, is intimately bound up with the impulse of Mercury. In addition to many other more profound indications that could be quoted, this is also expressed in the fact that in Christian times very often Mercury shrines were transformed into Michael sanctuaries.

In the Middle Ages, when the work of the demons of fear and terror connected with the Huns had erupted in the leprosy that afflicted the whole of Europe, a Mercury or Raphael age began (approximately from the ninth to the end of the twelfth century).[18] From the spirit of Mercury emanated the healing counterforce that manifested especially in such individuals as Francis of Assisi. Having lived initially in accordance with the old martial ideas of knighthood, he became a great healer and embodiment of love.[19] In his very person Francis of Assisi is like a historical picture of the transition from Mars to Mercury.

During the lifetime of Francis of Assisi (1182-1226) a new wave of Mongolian invasion began under his contemporary, another scourge of God, the terrible Genghis Khan (1162-1227) and his followers, once again drastically threatening the progress of human evolution as a whole. The age of Mercury and Raphael reached its culmination with Francis of Assisi, while with Genghis Khan an age of Mars and Samael began. During this age the transition from the Middle Ages to modern times, from the fourth to the fifth post-Atlantean era took place. It was an age when once again what might be termed the normal progress of human evolution was threatened by forces of destruction and turmoil.

*

An extensive literature about Genghis Khan and his empire appeared during the 1930s,[20] as though out of a sense of inherent facts that had a bearing on the immediate present or near future.[21] Although these books are all extremely informative and give thorough characterizations of the phenomenon, their full significance is only revealed when they are viewed in conjunction with what Rudolf Steiner discovered in his spiritual research and expressed in lectures given in 1916. Here he spoke about the deeper impetus underlying the Mongolian invasions and how these had been connected with efforts to distract and divert human consciousness from the path it is meant to follow during the fifth post-Atlantean era that was then about to begin.

If the consciousness soul is to evolve in the proper way during the 2,160 years of this fifth post-Atlantean era, mankind will have to develop two specific faculties. One of these, in contrast to earlier times, is the capacity to look with clarity at the sense-perceptible world, to set aside any visionary or fantastical elements when observing its realities; and the other, still to come in the future, is the ability freely to generate spiritual imaginations such as Goethe was beginning to develop, imaginations of the kind striven for in spiritual science. It was this normal course of evolution that Luciferic and Ahrimanic powers were seeking to disrupt. One strong impetus of which they made use to this end were the after-echoes of Atlantean times. It was an impetus that began before the beginning of the fifth post-Atlantean era and which was intended to play havoc with its progress. It came over to Europe from Asia.

'Essentially, descendants of the ancient Atlantean teachers were the ones who were working from a particular location in Asia,' said Rudolf Steiner. 'A priest was trained in a seership that allowed him a belated view of what the Atlanteans had earlier called "the Great Spirit". He was able to receive orders from the "Great Spirit" which he then passed on to an exceptionally strong, active and capable young man, Genghis Khan who, as a result of these orders, came to be known among his own people as the "great ruler of the earth". Through the priest came orders from the successor of the "Great Spirit" to Genghis Khan to seize all the power he could in Asia in order to spread through the world an influence that would lead the fifth post-Atlantean era back into a Luciferic form.'[22]

Extensive forces were concentrated to this end. 'Freely achieved spiritual imaginations were to be transformed into old, visionary imaginations. Every effort was to be made to lull human souls into a dreamy awareness of those imaginations instead of a free experience of them enlightened by the intellect. The forces obtained from Atlantis were to be imposed on the west in a way that would make its culture a culture of dreamy, visionary consciousness . . . All the unease resulting from the Mongolian invasions and everything connected with it that persists even to this day in the fifth post-Atlantean era . . ., all this unease signifies the grand attempt, emanating from the direction of Asia, to make the culture of Europe a "culture of visions", thus separating it off from the direction human evolution ought to be following . . .'

Rudolf Steiner described this in another way as well:[23] There existed a kind of descendant or successor of the 'Great Spirit' of Atlantis whose name still resounds in the Chinese *Tao*. 'This kind of descendant of the "Great Spirit" was concentrated over in the east where, in the tenth, eleventh, twelfth centuries, a certain Mystery cult evolved. Essentially, this Mystery cult was a form of renewal of the ancient *Tao* cult, not in the intellectualized form elaborated by the degenerate Chinese but in its original form. It renewed a form of initiation that enabled the priests to see the world of elemental spirits that lives and weaves directly beneath our own sense-perceptible world; the great, overall spirit became perceptible. Some priests in this revived Atlantean Mystery in Asia were initiated into the old Atlantean cult which, naturally enough, led to illusions, since it was out of place at that time.

'One of these priests became so highly developed . . . that he was able fully to comprehend the nature of the Atlantean impulse. He it was who conversed with that unlawful successor of the "Great Spirit". Over there in Asia this priest passed the *spiritual* inspirations he had received from the "Great Spirit" to an external, worldly power, that youth known to history as Genghis Khan . . . What the priest told Genghis Khan may be expressed in the following words: The time has come for the divine judgement to sweep across the face of the earth. You are the instrument through which this divine judgement is to come about; you must lead all the forces of Asia in fulfilling the divine judgement throughout the world.

'Similar aims had earlier provided the foundation for the campaigns of the Huns. Now the impetus given by this Asian priesthood inaugurated the Mongolian invasions which were intended to overlay European culture and make souls really believe in this divine judgement to such an extent that they would turn away from the earth and lose all inclination to return there. In this way earthly culture was to have been destroyed. This was the inner significance of the Mongolian invasions which swept over from Asia . . . and then came to nought in Europe through no external agency. That was the extraordinary thing, . . . that at the Battle of Legnica (in 1241, after the death of Genghis

Khan) the Mongolian hordes were not vanquished. They were the victors and yet for some unexplained reason they refrained from further incursions and returned to Asia. It is perfectly obvious that they had been met by a counterforce of a spiritual kind . . . '

The external explanation given (a miracle in itself!) is that news reached the Mongolians in Europe informing them of the death of Genghis Khan's successor in distant Mongolia. In accordance with Genghis Khan's decree, such a circumstance meant that all members of his clan, wherever they might be, must return to a grand council to decide on a successor, and this was supposed to be the reason why their victorious progress in Europe was broken off so abruptly.

Rudolf Steiner spoke of a deeper reason for the ending of the Mongolian invasions after the battle of Legnica in the thirteenth century.[24] He stated that the spiritual work cultivated by the Scholastics and the mystics at that time led to the development of a strong spiritual force that spread out over the whole of Europe, acting like a spiritual barrier which broke the Mongolian onslaught of atavistic Orientalism. This is obviously a most important view which may also be seen as an urgent challenge in our own day.[25]

In his lecture Steiner also added that because the impulses brought by the Mongolians were unable to make any headway externally in Europe 'they nevertheless remained in Europe in a kind of distillation during the fifth post-Atlantean era. Therefore, the cultural impulses coming from the east clearly contain . . . elements of what was to have been brought to Europe in the after-echoes of the Mysteries of the Great Spirit.'

A comparison may be drawn here with the spiritual advances made by Arabism in Europe in the Middle Ages after a similar retreat of the Arabs when they lost the battle against Charles Martel near Poitiers in 732. Mingled as it is with Luciferic and Ahrimanic impulses, the stream of Arabism is another cultural element that tends to work against what ought to be the normal progress of human evolution. However, this analogy is not intended to imply that Arabism might be comparable with the terribly destructive nature of Mongolian power.

The effect of the Mongolian impulse in the long term was intended to be a dimming of human consciousness, especially in the west. A wrong kind of visionary state was to have estranged human beings from the earth. The fact that this impulse was Luciferic was what primarily concerned Rudolf Steiner. He continued his description by showing that in the larger context of world history as a whole a balance was created against this Luciferic deviation by the discovery of America which took place in the normal course of evolution and established a counterweight to the activities of Genghis Khan. 'America had to be discovered so that human beings might come closer to the earth and be more and more filled with material substance so that their added weight would counteract the type of spiritualization striven for by the successors of the "Great Spirit".'[26]

In contradistinction to those Atlantean forces of Asia, however, this set in motion other forces, also stemming from ancient Atlantis, which in America worked on in the worst possible Ahrimanic form. These impulses originated in the Mysteries of Mexico and their successors, which covered a large part of the American continents. They were connected with the gold treasure later discovered in America which then seized hold of Catholic Spain.[27] We cannot here go into the many things Rudolf Steiner had to say on all these matters.

*

Attila was known to his people as the Heavenly Son[28] and the Chinese emperor was worshipped as the Son of Heaven. Out of the same ancient Atlantean mood and attitude to the world Genghis Khan also saw himself as the servant of the 'Ever-blue Sky', and this 'Ever-blue Sky', surely, is none other than a representation of the 'Great Spirit'. Genghis Khan harked back consciously to Attila, calling him his ancestor and deriving from him the legitimacy for his own rulership claims.[29] Known initially as Temujin, he called in 1206 a great council of all the tribes who were either subject to him or with whom he was allied. There the shaman Gökchu-Teb-Tengri - the son of another shaman, Munlik, who seventeen years previously had foreseen that Temujin was destined to become khan - declared that the 'Ever-blue Sky' had now commanded him to announce to the Mongolians that Temujin had been chosen to rule over all peoples and bear the name Genghis Khan. He was acclaimed ruler of the world, the 'ruler blessed by the Spirit of Light', as one historian called him, a most significant designation in view of the Luciferic grounding of his mission.[30] Perhaps either Munlik or Gökchu was the very priest mentioned by Rudolf Steiner as having provided Genghis Khan with his decisive impetus.

Now Genghis Khan proclaimed that he would lead the Mongolians to rule the world, calling his people the Mongols of the 'blue of heaven', a name that awakened their national pride.[31] Whatever their clan, thenceforth 'those who lived in yurts' felt uplifted by calling themselves 'Mongolians'. His every deed manifested 'the commands of the sky' and at the behest of the 'Ever-blue Sky' he set out to conquer the world.

99

The life of ancient Atlantis is very evident in the way the Mongolians lived without individuality in an entirely collective consciousness enclosed within the ties of blood in family, clan and tribe. It is the same 'compactness' already mentioned in connection with the Huns, and it is diametrically opposed to any kind of western consciousness. The whole of society was founded on kinship. Genghis Khan established what in modern terms might be called a 'fundamental law of the state' so that his realm might exist for all eternity. This 'Yassa' was founded on the tribal feeling and patriarchal social structure of the nomads. Crimes committed against kinspeople and against tribal discipline were heavily punished. This group consciousness lacking in any individuality was obviously the basis for the decadent, visionary clairvoyance which Rudolf Steiner said was to have been spread all over the west by the invasions of the Mongolian hordes. One expression of this atavistic consciousness was the Mongolians' picture language which appears to have moved from image to image rather than communicating in concepts.

Another trait of the Mongolians, their proverbial filthiness, fits in with this kind of consciousness. Centuries earlier than Genghis Khan the Chinese had already been calling their neighbours in Mongolia, Manchuria and Turkestan 'the filthy ones' or 'those who stink'. Uncleanliness was considered to be one of the chief virtues. It was treated with religious reverence and any urge to be clean was severely restricted by ritual prohibitions. The 'Yassa' contained the sentence: 'All is pure, nothing that exists is dirty,' and threatened the death penalty for those who bathed in rivers or washed their clothes. Furs had to be worn until they fell to pieces. There is a connection between physical cleanliness and the conceptual clarity of an alert consciousness; an atavistic, dreamy, visionary consciousness is abetted by squalor.

All this points to the mood of soul manifested by the Mongolian races of that time, an eastern mirroring of Atlantean traits closely bound up with the Luciferic element. This was the more inward aspect, and it revealed the essence of the impulse with which they strove to blanket the world. It was matched, however, by an equally strong outer side to their nature, and it is this outer side that is most often described. It might be termed their 'genius for organization', which came into play in the way they planned and carried out their wars as well as in the organization of their state. With the utmost discipline the concentrated power of the whole nation was made to serve the intentions of the central military and political leadership. On a grand scale a military and political strategy was developed which owed its success to that unquestioning and concentrated discipline.[32]

When these two sides are taken together it becomes obvious that the polarity on which the phenomenon of the Mongolians was founded was exceptionally far-reaching. Luciferic and Ahrimanic impulses complemented one another in a unique union. Instead of being kept apart and suspended in balance by a human middle element they were welded together to form an irresistible force. This in essence appears to be the phenomenon of Mongolianism, and seen in this light it confirms an experience often met with in history as well as in life, which is that the strongest attacks of Lucifer and Ahriman, especially on human consciousness, are achieved when these two powers work in concert. The successes of the Mongolians were made possible by the precise military and political organization and discipline with which they served an intoxicating Luciferic idea, and by the inspiring tempest of that Luciferic impulse reaching out from the past for which they provided support in superb military and state organization. Despite the terror which these successes still strike into our hearts, we cannot but remain utterly astonished at the power with which they were achieved. Genghis Khan conquered the greatest empire ever known on earth. His impulse was destructive and its terrible traces are indelibly recorded in history by rivers of blood and millionfold murder.

*

The Mongolians of Genghis Khan in the narrower sense were nomadic peoples stemming from Mongolia. In the wider sense, however, the term 'Mongolian' includes all peoples of Mongolian descent, especially the Chinese and Japanese. These, especially the Chinese, looked back to a very ancient, highly sophisticated culture. Like that of the nomads it, too, harked back to the echoes of Atlantis.[33]

The strongest planetary effect on the Mongolian race as a whole comes from Mars. Just as the Malayans are the Venus race, the Negro peoples the Mercury race, the Red Indians the Saturn race, and the Europeans or Aryans the Jupiter race, so are the Mongolians the Mars race,[34] by which is meant that it originally came into existence when certain Mars beings exercised their influence in the blood stream of these peoples. In this sense Rudolf Steiner characterized the Mongolians as having become hardened in their blood aspect, that aspect that gives external expression to the ego.[35]

Among the cultured Mongolian races the Mars character of the past is especially apparent in the Japanese. Their noble warrior caste of the

Samurai was founded on the ideals and virtues of chivalry culminating in the cult of the sword, of which it used to be said: 'The sword is the soul of the Samurai; if it is rusty, the soul is tarnished; if it is bright, the soul of the Samurai is also bright.' Even the name of the Samurai might be said to echo the Hebrew name of the archangel who accompanied the age of Mars: Samael.

Above all, however, the Mars character at its most typical is to be found among the Turanian nomads and the Mongolians of Mongolia itself. Fighting amongst each other these nomadic tribes wandered all over Mongolia. 'How could they have lived in peace' we read in one of the newer books about Genghis Khan, 'when pastures were growing ever more scarce and there was nothing beyond the border either? Restricting each other's freedom of movement on all sides, the hordes fought incessantly. They were driven to roam, but now they were forced to fight in order to do so. Or it could equally well be said that they roamed in order to fight. War for them was a part of life, indeed it was the very reason for existing. It was the normal state, whereas peace represented a disagreeable crisis. Some of the nomadic tribes of the Urals and the Altai mountains used but one expression for "to wander" and "to cut down with the sword"!' It would be hard to find a better description of the archetypal Mars nature of the Mongolians.

Genghis Khan united all these tribes under his rule, thus gaining the core of his subsequent empire. He directed outwards the combined force of his nomads who had hitherto been fighting one another. By means of an organizational miracle he pursued his aim of ruling the world. Military effectiveness depends on organization. The work of Mars is characterized by the combination of individual courage and devotion with the most efficient organization of the whole in which the strength of all the individuals is rolled together and used purposefully in the service of overall aims. Another important aspect is the right choice of aides, the positioning of suitable people in the higher and lower echelons of leadership. Since he possessed a profound understanding of his fellow men, Genghis Khan was able to achieve this brilliantly. All this gave the Mongolian army its immense force. In the truest sense of the word it was a national army: the people were an army and the army was the nation.

From Mars came the impulse for the grand strategy of the Mongolian campaigns which were preceded by systematic espionage in the lands to be conquered, as well as other careful preparation. Mongolian strategy proved superior to that of every other army of the time. Among the tactics they employed was the stratagem of pretended flight that tempted the enemy

102

into pursuit and thus lured them into ambushes. They also deceived the enemy into believing their numbers to be far greater than in fact they were, and above all they systematically spread terror and dread by instigating massacres and all kinds of other horrors. Thus they were tremendously successful in weakening their enemies with paralysing fear; their reputation for being unconquerable went hand in hand with fear of being overcome by them, since this was tantamount to annihilation. They wanted to appear as the tools of the 'wrath of God' so that any resistance would be abandoned as useless.

Another aspect of the Mars nature is the tendency to reduce every relationship to the formula of 'friend-foe' or 'for-against'. The Mars dynamic or Mars ethic means that I will keep faith with those who are on my side but will seek to destroy those who are against me.

Thus the Mars ethic involves not only courage, bravery, endurance, and the capacity to bear the most terrible hardships and privations, all of which the Mongolians possessed in the highest degree. It also denotes everything relating to the concept of 'friend'. As well as unshakeable military discipline in every war situation this includes 'comradeship', a capacity which the Mongolians had also developed in a high degree. Nine men together with a tenth as their commander made up the smallest unit of the army; they were bound together in life and death. It was better for them all to be killed than to abandon even one wounded man, and anyone leaving his comrades was subject to sentence of death without mercy.

Loyalty to those who had come to his aid, especially in his early beginnings, was one of Genghis Khan's characteristics. He never forgot and indeed created an unusual institution in connection with this, the title of *nukur*. This was awarded to men who earned it through the way they served him. They were relieved of taxes for all time, had permission to enter his yurt whenever they wished, were allowed to retain any booty they acquired and could nine times commit offences for which others were executed immediately.

Another significant aspect was the relationship of these peoples to the Mars metal, iron, which they revered in an almost religious manner. The Huns had also worshipped iron in all its forms, and 'Genghis Khan, like the earlier khans of the great Turkish empire, was revered as "the great smith of his people",' a designation signifying more than the merely abstract, figurative meaning it would have for Europeans. Iron in this context must be taken to include both the outer iron from which the weapons of war are fashioned and also the iron carried by human beings in their blood, the hardening of which, under the influence of certain Mars beings, we have mentioned as being one of the characteristics of the Mongolian peoples. The Mongolians practised an 'iron' discipline in war; the tablets on which the 'Yassa', Genghis Khan's law, was inscribed, were made of iron; in 'letters of iron' it was written in the head and heart of every Mongolian, from the lowest to the highest, where it remained for some time after the death of Genghis Khan, though not in all eternity, as he would have wished.

*

Genghis Khan focussed the energy of all the nomadic tribes of central Asia. In him Turan, the enemy of cultural advancement, grew to gigantic stature in the ghastly wishful dream of the nomads to turn the world into a single great steppe covered with the herds and yurts of roaming tribes. First of all he had to gather and unite the nomads, after which they would have had to rule over the cultured peoples of the earth. If such a thing had really come to pass it would have meant the death of these cultured peoples and thus of any culture at all in a higher sense. Needing their services, he raised individual members of cultured peoples, such as the Chinese or those of Islam, to elevated positions in his administration. But in the main he despised these cultures because they were too urban, too unmanly, too foreign. The Mongolian national consciousness he awakened in his people, and with which he opposed the ancient cultures, was without substance in a higher sense, and yet it existed as a force of terrible power. This force is the basic desire of the lower to dominate the higher, a desire that was deeply embedded in the nature of the Turanians. It is something that causes the most powerful forces of will to unfold and leads to the devising and application of most ingenious methods by means of which such dominion is to be achieved.

Thus from his point of view it was urgently necessary for Genghis Khan to cling to the nomadic way of life as the source of all his power and to anchor it firmly in the Mongolian peoples. Under his successors and descendants, however, this principle proved untenable. Since they had to live side by side with the cultured nations they began to absorb their customs and habits. This exhausted their wild and nomadic vital energy and the civilizing process became for them more disastrous than the inner feuds and bloody quarrels that finally broke the Mongolian empire some time after the death of its founder.

*

Just as there was only one 'Ever-blue Sky' and one 'Great Spirit', so there was to be only one ruler on earth, chosen by the Great Spirit. It was an attitude expressed in Genghis Khan's impressive formulation: *One* divine ruler in heaven and *one* great khan to rule the earth!

This was the spiritual foundation for the Mongolian desire for uniformity and power. In its service they placed the might of their Mars qualities, their organizational talent and their capacity to maintain a great state. All this was connected with the lack among nomadic peoples of any cultural creativity, a lack that had already been visible in the great Turkic empire of the fifth century.

Exemplary order reigned within Genghis Khan's empire; an end was put to robbery along the great trade routes, there was a postal system using mounted carriers, and trade developed freely. The *Pax Mongolica* covered an immense area. At the death of Genghis Khan and beyond, his realm stretched from Korea and the Yellow Sea to the Black and Arabian Seas. Communications were highly developed with a road network covering the whole empire that enabled the cultures of east and west to meet. The overcoming of distance achieved by European technology at the beginning of the twentieth century was anticipated in the thirteenth by the wild will forces of Genghis Khan and taken to its ultimate perfection in Kublai Khan's imperial organization.[32] Merchants using the route from the Genoese colony of Tanais on the shores of the Sea of Azov to China reported that it was entirely safe by day and night as a result of the *Pax Mongolica* or *Pax Tatarica*. Thus the thirteenth century saw world commerce made possible by the unnatural, superhuman forces of expansion developed by a primitive people on horseback. It was not to last long, however, and by the second half of the fourteenth century the unity of the European-Asian continent had collapsed once more.

As mentioned above, the organization of the Mongolian state reached its culmination in the realm of Kublai Khan (d. 1294) who was a grandson and successor of Genghis Khan. He ruled China and the Far East while the middle and western regions had already become relatively independent under other descendants of Genghis Khan.

Rudolf Steiner stated that Kublai Khan, too, was still influenced by the initiation discussed in connection with Genghis Khan.[36] At his brilliant court resided for many years the Venetian Marco Polo (1254-1324) whose book about *The Wonders of the World* for the first time described this remote Chinese-Mongolian realm. For a long time his tales met with disbelief, so fantastic and astonishing did they sound.

Kublai Khan had moved his residence from Mongolia to Peking, and his realm now achieved something like a synthesis of Mongolian organizational energy and talent with the culture of the Chinese. This entailed a watering-down of the wilder aspects of the Mongolian character and thus ultimately played a part in bringing about the end of Mongolian rule in China followed by the dissolution of the Mongolian empire as a whole. Meanwhile, however, conditions in Kublai's realm were truly remarkable in that they showed what a synthesis between the wild nature of nomadic Mongolians with the high culture of those of China was capable of achieving.

Descriptions of Kublai's realm reveal an exemplary administration, far-reaching social welfare and many other characteristics of a flourishing community full of social concern. Joachim Barckhausen considered that, measured against its power and extent, its technical and social institutions need not appear so very astonishing.[37] From the vantage point of the twentieth century it ought not to be too difficult to gain an idea of the capacities of a totalitarian state that makes full use of all its powers. The picture arising from Marco Polo's reports is of a tax system that is not overstretched and a state that endeavours to promote production and trade and allow the public purse to place commissions with industry and commerce. The court at Peking receives enormous revenues and functions as the heart of the realm, quickening its pulse by the exchange of goods. Social welfare is of a high standard. Anyone becoming poor through no fault of his own receives state support equal to his normal standard of living. Soup kitchens cater for the poorest classes. There is an obligation to provide labour for the state. 'Wherever there is a question of organization,' said Barckhausen, 'the Mongolians are exemplary. They bring a kind of Asian Prussian-ness to the Far East. With the help of an efficient policing system criminality is appreciably reduced . . .'

This ideal, realized by the Mongolian Chinese state under Kublai Khan, reveals nuances that remind us of the modern Chinese writer Ku Hung-Ming who described the significant elements of Chinese administration in connection with its ancient ideals.[38] Ku Hung-Ming compared the western, Christian question 'What is the highest purpose of the human being?' with that of the Confucian catechism 'What is the highest purpose of the citizen?' For him the highest purpose of the individual as a moral being is 'to be an obedient son and a good citizen'. He compared the Chinese person with a domestic animal, tame and lacking in individuality and thus easily led. A Chinese is an eminently social creature because the impulse to individuality has not yet dawned in him. In all seriousness Ku Hung-Ming therefore suggested that in order to escape from the strife of the western world, western people ought to be changed into true Chinese. Repeatedly and emphatically he challenged the western nations to tear up their Magna Carta of freedom and establish in its place 'a Magna Carta of loyalty such as we Chinese possess in our religion of the good citizen'.

All the impressive social structures of eastern Asia have grown and developed on this basis of the old pre-individual sense of community. The individual is embedded in the community as though in a large family. He is easily led (as at the more Chinese, passive end of the scale) and ready to make any sacrifice on behalf of the community (as at the more active end of the scale seen in the Japanese or the Tatar Mongolians). These community structures take absolutely no account of the individuality becoming aware of itself, and the western problem of the tension between the individual and the community is non-existent as far as they are concerned.

We have already mentioned that the Mongolians of Genghis Khan and his successors lost their vitality and perished as a result of their intense contact with their cultured neighbours. Finally the Chinese rose up successfully against their Mongolian overlords. With a proclamation beginning with the words 'These barbarians are created to obey and not to command a cultured nation' China began the attack, thereafter taking only a few months to shake off the yoke. In 1388 the Mongolians were beaten in Mongolia by a Chinese army. They relinquished the proud name of Mongolians given to them by Genghis Khan and henceforth once more called themselves Tatars.

Bloody feuds had already been going on for some time among the other, more westerly tribes of the Mongolian empire, especially between the Persian Il-Khans and the Russian Golden Horde. These feuds absorbed much energy and it is probably to them in the first place that Europe owes the fact that the Mongolians did not return after the battle of Legnica in 1241 or come back at any later date. Their dominion never stretched further westwards than their Russian realm.

The dissolution of the Mongolian realm took place in silence, almost uncannily. Hollowed out as though by termites the colossus still stood for a number of decades merely because in an Asia weakened by what had passed there was nothing to take its place. Finally, almost without any external inducement, it collapsed and fell to dust.

*

Something that points to deep secrets of human evolution is the fact that Buddhism found its way to the peoples we call Mongolian in the widest sense. This occurred in China in the first century AD, in Tibet in the seventh, and in Japan in the sixth. The Mongolian Tatars, however, only adopted Buddhism after the time of Genghis Khan.

Rudolf Steiner explained the spiritual realities lying behind this fact when he spoke of Buddha as having been the bearer of a divine entity who had been incarnated among human beings during the time of Atlantis when human bodies were not yet as dense as they later became. Because this was so, human beings came to know gods such as Thor, Odin, Balder and Zeus as companions on earth. Later, when the human form became ever more dense as it descended more deeply into the material world, these beings remained in the supersensible world and became invisible to human eyes.

'Those human beings who purified their more delicate bodies, by living in accordance with the instructions given by the initiates, went out in a certain way towards the gods. Thus, although they were incarnated in fleshly bodies, if they purified themselves they became capable of being overshadowed by a spiritual being who could not descend as far as a physical body . . . In this way Buddha became a vessel for Odin. The god named Odin in Germanic mythology appeared again as Buddha.

'Thus it is possible to say that much of what was secret in Atlantean times passed over into the message proclaimed by Buddha. What Buddha experienced was in harmony with what the gods had experienced in those spiritual realms and what human beings themselves had experienced when they still lived in those realms. When Odin's teachings reappeared they took little account of the physical plane apart from stressing that it is an abode of pain from which it is important to seek release. Much of what had been in Odin's being spoke through Buddha, and that is why Buddha's teachings met with the deepest understanding in those who were latecomers from Atlantis. Among the Asiatic population there are peoples who have definitely remained behind at the Atlantean stage, although outwardly, of course, they have kept pace with earthly evolution. In the Mongolian peoples much remains that comes from Atlantis; they are stragglers following on from the ancient population of Atlantis. The more stationary stream of the Mongolian population represents an inheritance from Atlantis and that is why the teachings of Buddha serve these people particularly well and why Buddhism has gained so much ground among them.'[39]

The significance of this fact is that the bellicose, aggressive Mongolian race of Mars, as though led by wise spiritual forces, has found a link with the Buddha, a being who is the very opposite of aggressive or warlike and instead emanates calm peacefulness, inwardness, compassion and love towards human beings. Far from being Mars-like, the Buddha is entirely Mercury-like.[40] It is as though his influence were intended to provide a healing antithesis for the Mars-like Mongolian peoples.* This places the phenomenon of Mongolian acceptance of Buddha in the context of the great link that exists in world evolution between Mars and Mercury. Mars must be transformed by Mercury; the effects of Mars must be 'healed' by Mercury. This belongs to the mission of Buddha as it was later fulfilled as a deed of redemption in the supersensible Mars sphere.[41]

The Mongolians of Genghis Khan adhered to the religion and magic of Shamanism in which decadent Atlantean forces were at work and which threatened the western world as a result of the Mongolian invasions. It is understandable that Genghis Khan himself remained faithful to these beliefs until the end of his life.

The final years of this wild conqueror, however, appear to have been surrounded in a strange way by the legends of Buddhism and Tibetan Lamaism. He approached the regions where they held sway in his campaign against the kingdom of Hsia, the north-eastern threshold to the highlands of Tibet. According to a Mongolian chronicle, Genghis Khan captured the daughter of the king of Hsia, a kind of Buddhist magician-priest and robber. 'He took her with him into his yurt, but she had learned the secret arts of the Tibetans from her father. As he lay with her for the first night she did a magic harm to Genghis Khan that thenceforth ailed him . . .'[42]

*Perhaps this may also lead us to the solution of a riddle rightly mentioned by Sigismund von Gleich on p.9 of his essay on 'Turanisch-mongolische Wesenszüge', op. cit. Here he points out the surprising contrast between the peaceful, almost feminine traits in the Chinese soul and the characteristics of the Turanian, Mongolian races. Perhaps this contrast indicates that very early on a 'Mercurial' counter-impulse went to work on the Martian, Turanian characteristics in the Chinese. This would also help us to understand another characteristic of the Chinese to which von Gleich also points, namely, their affinity with calculation and mathematical thinking on which their talent for commercial matters is founded.

In retelling this story recorded by a Mongolian prince of a later century who had meanwhile converted to Buddhism, Barckhausen pointed to its obvious symbolism: Tibet took revenge for the sacrilege committed against it and slew Genghis Khan. 'Some day in the future, when the yellow priests descend from the forbidden mountains, the whole of the Mongolian nation will suffer what their Khan suffered.' Expressing the great historical phenomenon in his own way, Barckhausen continued: 'The religion of Buddha has turned the Mongolians into powerless, defenceless devils. Because of it the once mightiest and strongest nation on earth is threatened with extinction today.'

*

There is a strange connection between the effects of the Mongolians under Genghis Khan and his successors and the discovery of America. On the one hand this discovery provided a kind of counterweight to balance out the deviation threatening humankind from the side of the Mongolians, but on the other hand it brought western humanity into contact with another deviation of the most terrible Ahrimanic kind.

Michael Prawdin,[43] for example, stated that despite all the fragmentation and civil strife that went on, while Mongolian dominion lasted the Asian-European continent remained united. By the middle of the fifteenth century, however, this had well and truly ended, and yet the stimulus received by Europe from the Far East during the brief period of unhindered trade and communication worked on. As all the land routes were now closed a sea route was sought. The great Khans had all disappeared and the Mongolian dynasties had long since vanished from the thrones of Asia 'but the search for the countries that their *Pax Tatarica* had opened up for the west, and that had been described by Kublai's courtier Marco Polo, led to the discovery of America by Europe.'

Thus what worked in the east linked up in the strangest manner with what worked in the west. The one led to the other in the pendulum swing from Luciferic to Ahrimanic pole. Rudolf Steiner showed how here, too, Ahriman and Lucifer worked together in close collaboration:

'Coming from the east the campaigns of Genghis Khan and his successors were intended to carry out a kind of divine judgement while in the west, in America, an atmosphere of wildest elemental forces was being prepared. In such things Ahriman and Lucifer work together in close collaboration. For example, the Europeans were not to come to America with feelings that were unselfish. They were to come with feelings of desire and covetousness, covetousness towards something about which they entertained a great many illusions. Later on there would be plenty of time to make these feelings more coarse, but initially they were surrounded by wonderful fantasies. The coarsening certainly took place when the Europeans found external riches in America in a manner that awakened their extreme covetousness, but initially all this was to take on a more idealized form. Once again we see in this the collaboration between Lucifer and Ahriman working, as ever, hand in hand.'[44]

Rudolf Steiner then continued to describe how Kublai Khan, himself still under the influence of the initiation that formed the starting point and stimulus for Genghis Khan's Mongolian invasions, was pleased to have at his court the Venetian Marco Polo: 'Marco Polo was thoroughly influenced while he was at the court of Kublai Khan where he wrote a book on *The Wonders of the World* that greatly stimulated the interest of the Europeans with regard to what might be found in the western hemisphere. His description of a magical land in the west[45] made people long to discover it. It was also one of the things that stimulated Christopher Columbus to undertake his voyage. Thus desires were awakened in a rightly fanciful kind of way. You see how cleverly things are arranged once you accept the fact that there are plans underlying world history, but that there are also plans that have to do with the forces of evil. If you view history as it is grasped these days you are really only coming to grips with its external aspect.' A mood was created 'that worked particularly in people's subconscious soul forces and was able to continue having its effect in cultural life.'

The fact that Marco Polo was a Venetian who could be used as a tool with which to bring about this swing of the pendulum towards the Ahrimanic pole may perhaps be seen as another symptom of what we said earlier about the special nature of Venice.

*

Mongolian rule in Russia, and especially its consequences, became very important for the west. Conquered by Batu, Genghis Khan's grandson, most of today's European Russia as well as the western regions of Asian Russia belonged to the khanate of the Golden Horde (from Mongolian *ordu*, meaning camp).

Rudolf Steiner pointed out that until the invasion by the Mongolians the social configuration in Russia showed a Germanic-Norman stamp.[46] If this Germanic-Norman element, with its social order based on clans who were relatively separate and independent of one another, had been the only influence, there would have been no possibility anywhere in Europe for a monarchy to come about, not even in Russia, where there was no thought of a state so long as society was formed by the Germanic, Norman influence. The idea of the clan had spread all over wide areas of Slav settlement where in today's usage the social atmosphere could have been described as democratic. At the same time, however, there existed a kind of 'longing to be without an overlord. This was based on the realization that centralized power is not really necessary for the creation of order in the world since in fact it tends to create only disorder. This feeling lived in these widespread Slav areas, and wherever the Norman-Germanic element reached there lived the idea of the clan linked by blood relationships.'[47]

The idea of monarchy came to Russia with the Mongolians. It came 'from the same direction as the Mongolians came although it had reached the more western parts of Europe earlier. What the Mongolians left behind them in Russia was the idea that a single ruler together with his paladins is supposed to run the state. This was the basic idea of monarchy taken from the khans. It had reached the western part of Europe earlier, and it was this Tatar or Mongolian idea that put together the state in Russia. Thus for a long time feudalism, on which western culture had been founded, had no influence in Russia. Here the idea of monarchy came straight in, missing out the stage of feudalism. In the west the monarchy was always disturbed by feudalism because the feudal lords were always fighting against the central monarch; they formed a counterforce to that of the monarchy.'[48]

Thus Russia became the kingdom of Muscovy, ordered after the manner of the Mongolians. It adopted the traditions of the Golden Horde, the Mongolian idea of the state and the capability of warlike organization. Russia was separated off from the west by the conquest; it was incorporated into the road networks and financial systems of the Mongolian empire. Thus, later, it did not invade the lands of Asia as a conqueror or bringer of the Cross but quite consciously as the successor of the Golden Horde. 'Moscow is the direct, legitimate heir of the Golden Horde', the Tsar is the successor of the Mongolian Khan. The designation 'white Tsar' signifies 'Tsar of the West' for white was the colour attributed to the west by the Mongolians.[49]

Since Mongolians and Russians intermarried, including the Tatar nobility with the Russian aristocracy, the Russian people became in a way infected with Mongolianism during the two centuries of their rule. In the words of Sigismund von Gleich[50] the Slavs became so accustomed 'to the abstract, despotic centralism of the Grand Khans that once they had shaken off the Tatar yoke they adopted its methods themselves. The white Tsars . . . as rulers of all the Russias took on these principles, in some cases handling them in masterly fashion: with Asiatic cruelty.' Finally, from 1917 onwards the white Tsars were replaced by the red party dictators of Communism: Lenin, Trotski and Stalin. Lenin himself was half Tatar. Especially after his death the mongolization of Bolshevism set in, a part of this being the transference of central emphasis to Asia, especially Siberia. Von Gleich's remark that Bolshevik Russia is in essence 'Turan' is very much to the point.[51]

In this way it came about that there are two polar opposite elements in Russia. On the one hand the Christian, Johannine element slumbered for centuries under the mantle of a rigidifying Byzantine church. Its goal is to lead the essence of Russia towards a lightfilled, Christian-Philadelphian future, but it is threatened by the second, opposing, element of Turanian Mongolianism. The relationship between the two is like that between Christ and Antichrist, Iran and Turan, or even angel and beast, of which it is said that they dwell side by side, sometimes at very close quarters, within the soul of the Russian individual.

*

We have already pointed out that the idea of monarchy which came with the Mongolians to Russia, where it replaced the older Norman-Germanic element in the social structure, 'had reached the more western parts of Europe earlier'.

Furthermore we quoted Rudolf Steiner as saying that after the battle of Legnica (1241), when the Mongolians flooded back to Asia, their influence 'nevertheless remained in Europe in a kind of distillation during the fifth post-Atlantean era'.

At least two influences on Europe are encapsulated here, one later, beginning in the thirteenth century, and one earlier, beginning, we may assume, in the fifth century in connection with the campaigns of the Huns. Of this earlier influence it is said that without it the idea of monarchy would never have taken hold in Europe. The later 'distilled' influence of the thirteenth century went in the same direction and it began, significantly, at the precise moment when important new beginnings of the centralized state had come into existence (such as the kingdom of Frederick II in Sicily and southern Italy) or were about to appear in the form of princely absolutism (as in the state of Philip the Fair, who destroyed the Order of the Templars).

Thus we find in the Mongolian influence a further source from which emanated forces that shaped and formed the centralistic state of more modern times, beginning with the phase of princely absolutism. All the better do we begin to understand a statement with which Rudolf Steiner obviously wanted to indicate these connections. People recognize, he said, that there has to be a social life of some kind, but they cling so strongly to the Mongolian idea of an all-powerful state because they have somehow 'concluded that whatever is not done by the state cannot be for the good of human beings.'[52] This important indication is further underlined by the way Steiner juxtaposed this 'Mongolian' idea of the state with Wilhelm von Humboldt's arguments on limiting the powers of the state.[53]

As we have seen, behind the Mongolian influence that still affects social life even in modern times there lies Atlantis with its grand vision of unity gazing heavenwards to the Great Spirit and with its priest-kings who ruled the peoples with unrestricted power like higher beings. The effects of this inheritance from the distant past are still felt even in our most recent centuries. Moreover, having been present in Mongolian times, the impulses coming from Mars also live on, transformed, in the centralized states of modern Europe. Since their beginnings in the Renaissance, these states have been formed essentially to suit the requirements of their armies.

*

In another lecture Rudolf Steiner again spoke about the campaigns that brought the Mongolians from Asia to Europe (and also about those of the Turks).[54] On this occasion it was the removal of the Pope to Avignon in 1303 which he connected with these events. As we have seen, the Pope's removal to Avignon signified a strong breach in the medieval universalism of the papal Church which had to give in to the new might of the nationalistic impulse growing in France, the impulse of the nation state that now made its entry into history. Whatever it was that the Mongolians brought with them to Europe began to work together with the monarchic, centralistic impulse. The two appear to be linked in a hidden way. Steiner added that there was an element like a force of nature both in the nationalistic impulse arising initially in France and in the influences brought in from Asia by the Mongolians and by the Ottomans.

Here, too, as in the discovery of America, an east Asian, Mongolian impulse worked together with a western impulse coming in this instance directly from France, behind which lay, however, an ancient American impulse. This and the Mongolian impulse both hark back or are related to the same Atlantean source. Metamorphosed in numerous ways, what came from that source appeared again at the end of the Middle Ages because the fifth post-Atlantean era was dawning, and it is with such elements that this era will have to come to grips.

There was, however, one critical difference between the new centralized states in the west and the social structure of the Mongolians. For many centuries in the west there was a complete absence of any community welfare such as had been so highly developed in the Mongolian, Chinese realm of Kublai Khan. European 'individualism' worked against such arrangements, however centralized and well-organized the states may have been. The consequence in recent centuries has been the emergence of what Carlyle described as 'anarchy plus a policeman'. This formulation is quoted with glee by Ku Hung-Ming because it expresses a situation in which he perceives a lack of any effective moral force[55] such as had lived in the ancient, community-oriented society of China. That society, however, lacked the forces of individuality.

*

In the year 434 Attila became king of the Huns. In 1175, after the death of his father, Yesugei, Temujin began the campaigns that were later, in 1206, to make him Genghis Khan, ruler of the greatest empire in history. Approximately seven-and-a-half centuries separated Attila and Genghis Khan. A further similar period brings us to the twentieth century. Such calculations may appear arbitrary, but the fact remains that in the first third of this century the great Genghis Khan was remembered in a special way in eastern Asia while in the west there seemed to be an increasing awareness of the inner relevance of such things. A flood of literature about Genghis Khan appeared, the inner topicality of which resounded with considerable force both in the historical and in the more fictional works.[56]

For example Michael Prawdin wrote at the end of 1935:[57] 'Far away and long-forgotten by the world had been the tradition of Genghis Khan. The name of the greatest conqueror of all time awoke only dim memories of a bogey from a long-gone era. But now we discover that the figure and tradition of Genghis Khan has been kept alive in Asia all along; it is now becoming a threatening vision of the future as the peoples of Asia begin to stir once more. The Chinese regard the Yüan, the dynasty of Genghis Khan's successors, as their emperors; the linen shirt of the great Mongolian conqueror is preserved in Petersburg like a sacred relic; Japan is seeking to prove that Genghis Khan was a Japanese nobleman . . .' In Mongolia, Prawdin continues towards the end of his book, a legend has long been circulating: 'When the most durable thing on earth, the kingdom in the north and the kingdom in the south, falls to dust, and when the white Tsar in Russia and the Son of Heaven in China disappear, then will a new Genghis Khan arise and create a new Mongolian empire.'

A similar version of this legend was told by a traveller in Afghanistan in 1938:[58] 'An Afghan dignitary gave me the following version of the Genghis Khan prophecy: "When the realm of the last white Tsar is destroyed Genghis Khan will come again." The people here also believe in the appearance of an Anti-Christ.'

The same theme is expressed in a different mode by Anton Zischka:[59] 'Mongolia is forgotten and without significance today, but the forces that drove Genghis Khan live on in Japan. In no other language have as many biographies of the great conqueror been written. Japan knows that in the empire of the great Mongolian ruler all the peoples of Asia lived side by side, that in his realm all religions were permitted, and that he was familiar with every Asian culture . . . Japan knows that in the eternal struggle between Europe and Asia Genghis Khan's forward thrust was the mightiest . . .'

APPENDIX

A Consideration of the Historical Development of 'Politics'

1. General

The term 'politics' as a social or historical concept has been taken to mean many things during the course of history.

For a long time, though not originally, it denoted a sphere of social life that could be clearly distinguished from cultural or spiritual, religious, scientific or artistic life on the one hand and from economic life on the other. More recently, however, it has taken on a much wider meaning, so that it is almost synonymous with the concept of social life in general. Applying the concept of 'politics' in this wider sense makes it possible to politicize the various areas of social life, such as science, by promoting their development in a way that will best serve society as a whole. In a similar way individuals can be 'politicized' by being encouraged to use all their thinking, feeling and will consciously and responsibly in the service of the community at large. The means by which individuals or specific areas of social life might be thus 'politicized' in this general sense are, however, left entirely open.

There is no reason why 'politics' should not be seen in this entirely general way so long as it is done consciously. The concept of 'politics' is then as old as any form of human society or community, even those of the ancient theocracies such as that of Atlantis, for they were all social in some way or other.

This example shows, however, that over-expansion of its content deprives the concept of its validity and of its particular nuance. It then becomes necessary to look for a new designation for what was contained in the narrower concept of 'politics' since what this narrower concept used to express still continues to exist.

For this reason, amongst others, we prefer to use the concept of 'politics' in its previous, narrower sense so as to distinguish it clearly from the generalized usage that includes the wider social dimension or indeed society as a whole.

With this clarification we hope to preempt any misunderstandings that would have arisen in the minds of readers if they had assumed us to be applying the concept of 'politics' in the wider sense.

*

'Politics' in the narrower sense has to do with the formation of a sphere of society concerned with the state and with the rights of individuals. It is a separate sphere representing only this aspect of social life and having its own character and structure. 'Politics is essentially to do with rights,' was how Rudolf Steiner put it.[1]

Therefore it was only able to come fully into its own once the age of the ancient theocracies had ended, for only then did the rights or state element of society arise in the sense to which we are referring here. As we saw earlier,[2] the theocracies were not finally replaced and overcome until the time of ancient Greece. The Trojan War was the epoch-making event in this connection. The words 'politics' and 'political' stem from the realm of the city-state of Greece, the *polis*. *Polites*, the citizen, was a fully-fledged member of one of these city-states. Further derivations are the adjective *politikos* and the feminine noun *politike*. Even in the origin of the word we find the connection with the city-states of ancient Greece and thus with the fourth post-Atlantean era. This in itself points to the fact that the concept of 'politics' can only be properly comprehended in connection with a particular evolutionary stage of human consciousness.

'Politics' in the narrower sense does not arise so long as the stimulus for social deeds and social leadership comes from higher realms through supersensible consciousness, as it did in the ancient theocracies, rather than out of any personal, human impulse.[3] 'Political' life only begins in earnest when human beings grasp and shape social life out of their own personal incentives, emotions and considerations.

If we did not make this distinction we might be tempted to speak of 'divine politics' as well as of human politics. We ought to sense, however, that such an expression, unless it is meant comparatively or figuratively, has no inner justification, since the divine sphere is situated above the political sphere. In ancient times the life of human beings, including the social aspect, was guided out of this higher sphere.

To define 'politics' correctly we have to distance it from the priestly, theocratic element. The priests in ancient times gave their dispensations neither out of human, intellectual considerations nor out of the realm of human desires or 'kama'. Their actions were free of 'kama'.[4] All their impulses and goals, and also the strength with which they acted, stemmed from a supra-personal connection with the spiritual world and spirit wisdom. On this rested their unlimited authority.

In early lectures[5] Rudolf Steiner spoke about the role of 'kama' (not to be confused with 'karma') in human evolution. It is the soul-quality of desire living in the heart and the warmth of the circulating blood; human beings have it in common with warm-blooded animals in whom it manifests in every possible way. In addition to its passionate side it also has another, opposite aspect, for it is that in human beings which can lead them to higher worlds if it is purified through catharsis.[6]

In ancient times those who were called to be leaders had to achieve a purification of their astral body by going through catharsis in initiation so that their personal passions would not have a destructive effect on the order of society. During the course of this process they came into contact with the supra-personal wisdom out of which they were able to guide social life; they brought into the world the impulses of the spiritual world, the wishes of the gods.[7]

Another way of expressing this would be to say that the principle of leadership in ancient times required that the individuals who were to lead should, in a greater degree than those who were led, have succeeded in overcoming the consequences of the Fall within themselves. They were responsible for guiding those still strongly influenced by it who were caught up in the less pure aspects of earthly life and governed by the desires of their lower nature. This throws light on another remark by Rudolf Steiner in which he spoke of the task of certain ancient initiates as being 'to form the state and consolidate the passions.'[8]

Notes recording a further lecture mention the Vedanta schools of ancient India: 'In these schools the question of karma was considered in a sphere that was free of emotions. Thus thoughts were purified of passion. This was a way of studying the intrinsic laws of the universe without any emotional distortion; it was what is called catharsis.'[9]

Out of this sphere it was possible, for example, to regulate the ancient caste system in a manner that befitted objective karmic situations, and it is also the sphere of which an echo still resounded strongly in Plato's *Politicus.*[10] Plato thought that only those who loved wisdom should be rulers and he attributed what he considered to be the unsatisfactory social situation of his time to the fact that statesmanship and love of wisdom were not going hand in hand.[11]

All this characterizes a period that we could describe as having been 'pre-political'.[12]

With the passing of time, however, the political element emerged to the degree that the ancient wisdom of the east, the attitude to knowledge and the will to fulfil the behests of the spiritual world decreased. The spiritual world withdrew, becoming veiled in darkness and leaving human beings to fend for themselves. Thus the human ego, the psychological personality, began to evolve on the basis of personal passions and emotions, personal love of power and personal tyranny, in other words on the basis of everything that generates strife, enmity and opposition in which people become personally engaged.

In the overall context of cultural history the ancient Indian name for this would be the *rajas* era which forms the transition from the old *sattva* era of light to the *tamas* era of darkness. Through *sattva* human beings are brought into contact with wisdom and goodness of every kind, whereas the *tamas* quality binds them to the world of the body. Between these, in the quality of *rajas*, people live in their passions and are filled with a thirst for existence. In world history the third post-Atlantean era belonged to the *sattva* culture while the fifth belongs to the darkness of *tamas*. Between these lay the fourth post-Atlantean era, that of the *rajas* quality.[13] It was the age in which the political element was born in the soul sphere of emotions and passions, both noble and not so noble, beginning in ancient Greece and reaching its culmination in Roman times.

It is noticeable how the two poles of human soul life began to pull apart. On the one hand there was the personal wish for power and might, the desire for fame, glory and respect; and on the other there was personal cleverness, cunning and calculation, the element of thought that serves aspirations founded on passionate desire.[14] This dual character is typical of politics in which the personality becomes aware of itself and grows strong. The result is an extremely colourful world, for the light of the spirit - although only shining through the clouded human soul element - is mirrored in many colours.

*

The fundamental forces of the soul are sympathy and antipathy.[15] The effects of these are to be found everywhere in politics in the basic meaning attached to the contradistinction of 'friend-enemy', two polar concepts by means of which human beings, typically ego-centric, establish relationships with the world around them in accordance with values arrived at in answering the question 'What's in it for me?' Quite rightly, therefore, the friend-enemy equation is regarded as a typical characteristic of politics. It functions in a Mars-like, bellicose fashion on the one hand through power and on the other through cleverness, cunning and deception of one's opponent. Politics, war, power and cunning are all closely related.

Much of this was expressed by Rudolf Steiner in the discussion mentioned above (although other statements he made on that occasion are less easily understood and should, perhaps, be allowed to stand as open questions):

'Politics is a secondary product of world history. It came about simply because primitive, perhaps highly unattractive, although entirely honest, power structures gradually adopted war as the way for human beings to function with one another. Instead of saying that war is the continuation of politics by other means, it would be more exact to point out that politics is modern warfare lifted up into the cultural realm. War today depends on duping the enemy by creating situations that lead him astray. Every avoidance tactic and all the things that are not direct attacks are founded on duping the opponent. Any commander will be praised the more when he succeeds in duping the enemy. This is politics, war transferred into the sphere of culture and spirit. All the same categories are found in politics as in war.

'You could say that we ought to strive to overcome politics everywhere, even in politics. The only correct politics will be when everything involved in it takes place in legal forms. This will then be the state founded on the law.'[16]

2. Aristotle on the Human Being as zoon politikon

In his *Politics* (I,2) Aristotle famously described the human being as *zoon physei politikon*.[1] This could be translated as 'by nature a creature of the state', or 'by nature a creature made for society', or even 'by nature a political creature'. In any case it is obvious that here, right at the beginning of its evolution, the word *politikos* was still very close to the entirely general meaning of 'belonging to society in general', although it had a special nuance to which we shall come in a moment and which is its most important aspect. This generalized meaning also appears in the *Historia animalium* (I 1, 11) where *zoa politika* are listed as being, among others, 'the human being, the bee, the wasp, the ant and the crane' because they join forces in undertaking common tasks. Finally, in the passage in the *Politics* already quoted, the human being is seen with the bee 'and any creature living in swarms or herds' as *zoon politikon*; but he is more *zoon politikon* than these because he has language and a sense of good and evil.

Since Aristotle regarded human beings together with certain animals as being *zoon politikon*, even though he also distinguished between them, we can feel justified in pointing out that the word *zoon* signifies not only 'creature' or 'living creature' but also 'animal'. The word has a 'zoological' aspect, and this nuance must also be included in an understanding of the description of the human being as *zoon politikon*. Rudolf Steiner did this when he mentioned that Aristotle had formulated 'the most comprehensive and penetrating concepts' which succeeding centuries had had to ponder and with which even today's thinking had not yet come fully to grips. Towards the end of the lecture in question Steiner spoke of the 'politicizing of the conceptual world' which especially the Romans had achieved. He then contrasted Aristotle with the Roman attitude which, especially in the *civis* concept, had placed the human being into human society 'in a political and juridical manner':

'Aristotle still spoke of *zoon politikon*; he still linked the political with the *zoon*, the animal. This was as yet an entirely different kind of thinking, an imaginative kind! It was not a political way of thinking; it did not yet politicize concepts.'[2]

This ability of Aristotle to think imaginatively and grasp the true essence of things, because he thought about the political element in a non-political way, enabled him to bring the political society in which human beings live into juxtaposition with the element that lives in the animal, or in which the animal lives. In keeping with this is the fact that Aristotle described the human being as *zoon physei politikon*, meaning that the human being is 'by nature' *zoon politikon*, or that he is *zoon politikon* especially on account of his physical, bodily nature which, in turn, is also what makes him a creature who is related to the animals.

At the most basic, physical level political life in the Aristotelian sense includes everything required to fulfil the needs of life, in other words the economic processes. There are certain economic processes even in the animal world. Rudolf Steiner spoke of the 'economy of sparrows or swallows' in which nature offers the products to which the individual animal helps itself. Human beings also make use of this sphere of animal economy, although they must, of course, rise above it.[3]

In the narrower political sense described above there is also an element that demonstrates the kinship between the human and the animal, the world of 'kama' or passion, the element of the political. This may appear in the royal form of the lion, pure embodiment of the middle, heart and breast system of the human organism, or in tiger or fox, bear or Roman she-wolf.

In so far as human beings live in the element of their urges and desires, the element in which they are related to the animals, they are existing in accordance with their 'species', their physical aspect, which is not yet their fully human aspect. The latter can only come entirely into its own when the individual ego awakens in each one.

All this is alive in Aristotle's vivid and many-facetted description of the human being as *zoon politikon*. It states that as a species human beings are political creatures. The adjective *physei* emphasizes this while also pointing to the fact that it is not 'by nature', not merely as creatures of nature, but by unfolding their higher, real human element, that human beings also belong to, or can enter into, another order, one that is higher than the merely political order.

The physical aspect of the human being is the foundation for a justified and necessary political order in Aristotle's sense. The aspect of human beings that makes of them a species, the urges and desires which are bound to their physical nature, are what might be called the 'material' with which the political order works, seeking to keep it on a medium level where it can mould and discipline it. Terrible consequences follow, however, if this 'material' strives to become the master or wants to step beyond the bounds of the political sphere and put its stamp on the whole of the social organism.

If this happens, the truly human element withdraws little by little to the extent that the individual human being, endowed with a human ego, is swallowed up by a collective 'species'. The central social problem is the question as to what can be done to ensure that the beneficial forces at work in each individual can also come into their own in society at large.

Historically this problem has been brought to the fore with a vengeance by Marxism. As a result of Marxism wide areas of the population have come to believe that genuine human evolution does not require the opinion of the individual, nor even what lives in each human being, but only the social reality that exists in the collective, i.e. in the economic sphere, or whatever rises up from the depths of economic necessity. 'This', said Rudolf Steiner, 'was precisely the contrast to modern proletarianism at which I arrived in my *Philosophy of Freedom*[4] which demands that everything should be founded on the human individual to whom these modern proletarian ideas attach no significance because they want to see human beings merely as social animals, creatures forming a society.'[5] We can see how the *zoon politikon* of Aristotle played into this sequence of thoughts. On the other hand it is understandable that in Bolshevism, which has perfected Marxism, the human being has been most systematically downgraded to a collective 'species' so that the 'animal' becomes the master.

The human being in his ego is at home in the spiritual, cultural sphere. This is the most fundamentally 'human' sphere in the social organism. From this sphere the human being endowed with ego, and as a participant in the objective reality of the spirit, creates a realm of truth, beauty and goodness. Only this pole of the social organism, out of its own resources, by fructifying, nourishing and kindling the social order as a whole, can banish the threat posed by the necessarily passionate, 'animal' character of the political and the economic spheres. A healthy social life is only possible if the individual spirit of the human being can work in suitable ways in all the spheres of the social organism, filling them with truly human essence.

If this could be achieved it would mean that social life would be de-politicized, when to be 'politicized' is meant in the sense of an unjustified flooding of the whole social organism by the political, state sphere in the narrower sense of the word.

3. The Role of Politics in Society

The tendency to politicize life in the above-defined sense, the inclination to consider and deal with almost every realm of life first and foremost from the point of view of politics and the state, began to assert itself when the political aspect as such came into being, which was when a separate legal, political, state aspect of society began to appear during the fourth post-Atlantean era, especially among the Romans. In *Volume I* we discussed the virtuosity with which the Romans politicized the religious life, thus causing all its solemnity and sacred force to dwindle in the same degree as it became a useful tool in Roman politics. The Roman she-wolf devoured the spiritual light for the sake of external political power.

Later on it was the Roman Church that made of Christianity not only a legal[1] but also a political entity, thus estranging it from its true essence. The Roman Church itself became a grandiose political institution achieving a mastery of politics which often superseded that of the 'secular' powers. This mastery of political power is linked to a deep kinship between the Roman Church and the political genius of the Romans.

For the French people, too, politics has become second nature. They regard everything under the sun from political points of view and have also mastered politics for centuries as their most fundamental capacity. In the French, the people of the 'Latin' culture, the fundamental tenor of the fourth post-Atlantean era lingers most strongly.

124

A new wave of 'politics' poured over Europe at the beginning of modern times, the fifth post-Atlantean era, in connection with the culture of the Renaissance in which many other elements of Antiquity were also revived. The figure of Machiavelli was symptomatic of that age. Rudolf Steiner said of him:

'You need only consider a phenomenon of the Renaissance such as Machiavelli and you will find in him a symbol in human form for the whole way in which thought life began to become political. Machiavelli is an expression, a manifestation of thought life that has become political. He is a mighty spirit, and yet under the pressure of the powers of which I have been speaking' (the powers of Lucifer and Ahriman) 'he entirely revived the attitudes belonging to the pagan times of Roman Antiquity. The proper historical way to look at Machiavelli is to see him as typical of many who thought as he did. He expressed powers that wanted to rush forward with retarded atavistic forces, Luciferic forces. If things had gone according to his wishes the whole of Europe would have become engulfed in politics.'

Steiner then continued by pointing out that the forces wanting to rush forward were impeded by others, the forces of normal evolution. He juxtaposed 'a purely political figure, a figure such as Machiavelli, who wanted to make all human thinking political' with another, almost his contemporary: Thomas à Kempis.[2]

In addition to 'making the life of thought political', Machiavelli was also typical of his age in wanting to make moral matters political, which was tantamount to making them hollow. This is what has been known as 'Machiavellism' down the centuries.[3] It is the inclination to replace other values by political expediency, making this the yardstick by which the political usefulness of everything else is measured. It has been an integral part of political and state life since the Renaissance.

*

The process of political encroachment in recent centuries must also be regarded in other connections. The old medieval mood of spirituality and religion had encompassed and carried people as whole human beings, but as this mood weakened and became powerless and decadent a kind of division began to take place in human souls. Thinking became intellectual and abstract and thus lost its close connection with the human will which it therefore no longer fired or directed. The will lost its firm orientation towards thinking, a situation which Rudolf Steiner formulated as 'thinking devoid of will, will devoid of thinking'. 'Because thinking and knowledge became so abstract, the will became dependent on emotions and purely personal instincts.' Thus, over the last three to four centuries 'egoism gradually became the decisive factor' in social life.[4] It is therefore understandable that as a result of the withdrawal and darkening of the spirit in recent centuries the realm of social activity, too, should have fallen victim to the emotions and passions of political egoism, both that of individuals and of groups.

This brings us to yet another important aspect of social life that must be recognized: As spiritual and cultural life grows ever more abstract and intellectual, its increasing impotence also becomes a factor in the social sickness of modern times.

One of the consequences of the impotence of spiritual, cultural life is the dominance of the political element (in the narrower sense) over cultural and economic life and also, conversely, the dominance of the economic sphere over political and cultural life. This constitutes a disorder of the archetypal, healthy social order founded in the nature of the human being and in the hierarchy of values. It is a social sickness or, mechanistically expressed, a disturbance of the social equilibrium, and it began to take its effect noticeably in the age of absolutism beginning around the seventeenth century.

By recognizing the fact that the increasing dominance of the political element is the result of the weakening of spiritual, cultural life as it grew ever more intellectual, we are avoiding the onesided historical error of blaming politics *per se*. We recognize that the spread of the political element is inextricably bound up with the tragedy inevitably connected with the evolution of the human ego which has been taking place especially in more recent times.

To transform the dominance of the political element in social life and confine it within the bounds defined earlier will only be possible to the degree in which the higher spiritual nature of human beings shining in their true ego can be made fruitful for this social life and become its guide and builder. If this could be achieved it would be the right way to overcome the dominance of politics in social life; it would be a deed founded on genuine social insight.

Plato said: 'Human generations will not escape from calamity unless either the true and genuine philosophers rule the state or the powerful and mighty are led by the gods to a genuinely philosophical attitude.' Although this harks back to former times of rule by initiates, it is nevertheless a statement that points very much to the future.

In different words Rudolf Steiner meant much the same when he said: 'These questions concerning public life will certainly become questions of knowledge removed from the atmosphere of sympathy and antipathy within which they are confined today by the vast majority of people. However, it will not be majorities that decide these things . . . '[5]

To act socially on the basis of genuine spiritual insight would then no longer constitute 'politics' in the traditional sense; it would mean 'politics' in the new sense becoming wise, beneficial and truly human rather in the way described by Rudolf Steiner in the phrase 'the removal of politics from politics'. There would be a kind of 'sacrifice of the snake' (as in Goethe's tale of the Snake and the Lily) for the good and increasing health of social life that has been made sick by the wrong kind of 'politics'. The Snake sacrificed itself to become a bridge over the river (which, as we shall see, is also the 'river of passions'), linking one bank with the other. Once this has taken place the kingdom of true humanity will begin, the kingdom of the golden, silver and bronze kings of the story.

For this to happen the 'merely personal' (which is so closely bound up historically with the coming into being of 'politics') will have to become supra-personal in a new sense. This has been the aim of the more hidden Christian impulses since the time of the esoteric communities of Christendom. As Rudolf Steiner put it: 'Everything arising from the Christian principle of initiation had by its very nature to work in an impersonal way. The personal element has always brought strife to humanity and it would do so even more strongly in the future . . . '[6]

4. 'The State and the Fall.' The Christ-Impulse

The question as to whether the existence of the state, or the political community, is connected in any way with the Fall is an old one, and there have been two opposing views about it.

Among those who regarded the state as a direct consequence of the Fall was Augustine, although some believe that this reading of what he meant has been based on a misunderstanding. The other view, that the state would have existed had the Fall never taken place and, indeed, that it came first, was held above all by Thomas Aquinas.

The first point to be made here is that in applying concepts of political community or state arising in later, historical, times to the dim beginnings of human evolution, both views fail to recognize the entirely different form of existence prevailing (in Lemurian times or before) when what

127

we call the Fall took place. For the first time since the days of the ancient myths mankind once again now has the opportunity to hear, through spiritual science, about that different form of existence. In consequence we find that both views contain an important core of truth pointing to spiritual realities.

Following Aristotle, Thomas Aquinas assumes human beings to be social by nature, unable to survive alone and needing to live in a community. Therefore, even in a condition of innocence, human beings lived together in communities. The state is not a consequence of sin; it is not an invention of the devil or a makeshift arrangement resulting from the Fall. Therefore there is neither need nor possibility for deliverance from the laws of the state to lead to liberty, since the order of the state is identical with the order of nature which is strengthened rather than destroyed by redemption.[1]

This view rightly assumes that even without the Fall, i.e. without the temptation of Lucifer, human beings would have been and remained social creatures. Indeed, they would have been particularly so, since without the Luciferic temptation they would have lacked any strongly-developed individuality or will of their own and been capable only of bowing down to the will of the gods. Thus they would have been social beings only, nothing more.

It is a consequence of the Fall that human beings gradually developed the consciousness we have today which separates them off from the external world and from the souls of their fellows. This alone makes possible the relationship between people that is fitting for the earth, namely, a measure of distance between individuals. In this connection Rudolf Steiner described the way in which human beings, not yet endowed with individual egos, related to one another in the conditions of old Moon, which preceded those on today's earth. 'Human beings did not interact with one another as they do today on earth because, in a way, they were too close to each other. During the time of old Moon the wish of one human being worked on in those around him. Human beings sensed each others' will, and the spirits of the higher hierarchies saw to it that this took place in the correct manner.'[2]

Thus the view that before the Fall human beings were social creatures living in community is more to the point than even the most radical exponents may have realized. The human being was, indeed, *zoon politikon*, a 'social animal'.

The opposite view, that regards the state as a consequence of the Fall, is evidently more concerned with what is meant in a more specialized and concrete sense by the political life of the state. This view links the political community very closely with the consequences of the Fall, and this, too, is justifiable. The state can, and indeed must, be regarded as an institution that protects the individual against his fellows in so far as they have within them all those egoistic, antisocial urges and desires, criminal tendencies and so on which are, after all, nothing other than consequences of the Fall of human nature.

It was along these lines that Vladimir Soloviev was thinking when he wrote about the military, an institution most intimately bound up with the functions of the state organism: 'There was as yet no such institution when innocent Abel was slain in anger by his brother Cain. Wisely fearing that the same fate might also befall Seth, good guardian angels mixed clay, copper and iron, and formed of the mixture a soldier and policeman; and so long as the feelings of Cain have not departed from human hearts the soldier and policeman will be not evil but good . . .'[3]

The final phrase is evidently aimed at views, such as those of Tolstoy, which held that the power of the state, with the necessary force it had to use, was intrinsically 'evil'. Obviously the state as such can no more be called 'evil' on account of its having to hold in check the consequences of the Fall than can a medicine prescribed by a doctor to cure an illness.

It is the task of the state to counteract excessive passion and egoism and protect individuals against their fellows so long as *homo homini lupus*, or man is a wolf to other men, in order that both the individual and the community may find a place where they can develop relatively undisturbed, and so that a social life can be made possible at all. Passions can, of course, only be truly transformed and purified by means of education and self-development, i.e. out of the powers of the cultural, spiritual life. Within the legal or state sphere it can be no more than a matter of containing the worst excesses of the Fall by means of external force against those who, like criminals, are unfree in their own urges and desires. The less a person can master his own desires and urges the more does he require to be led from the outside, by external laws and regulations. This is obvious in the case of children but it is also so in the case of criminals, and this applies to all human beings in so far as they cannot rise above the sphere of external constraint through moral development.

While the above refers more to those who are governed, the nature of the state and its relationship to peoples' passions can also be discussed more from the point of view of those who do the governing: The state provides a 'legal' framework within which human passions can be satisfied by means of wielding legitimate power or occupying positions of honour, or by the achievement of ambitions. This diverts the passions into channels where they are less harmful for the life of the community or can, indeed, be of service to it. This is where change by means of long-term social education could begin. Perhaps it is also what Rudolf Steiner meant by saying that the state must 'consolidate the passions'. It digs a channel for them into which they can pour and along which they can flow.

Thus does the state become 'the river of the passions'.

In all this the life of government, law and politics is revealed in its true position lying between the realm of the spiritual, cultural life, through which people meet higher, supersensible worlds, and the realm of economics and commerce through which they are related to the sub-human, physical world. The life of the state and politics, directly concerned with human beings, lies between these two. In its middle position it could be compared with the soul realm to which it is related, which lies between the higher and the lower nature of the individual. Just as the soul can devote itself to higher things or be ensnared by what is lower, so is it with the state and politics. It can serve the spiritual pole of the social organism and the human being, or it can fall prey to the lower nature, even though at a certain level it dominates this nature. Or it can seek to rise above even the higher sphere in order to dominate that too, instead of serving it. Then power becomes evil. It is not evil in itself but it becomes evil when it is misused. The danger of misuse is the greater the less the spiritual, cultural life is able to fulfil its elevating function within the social organism as a whole.

*

In the light of this knowledge about the connection of politics and state with the Luciferic temptation, that great event in human evolution, we can also understand certain remarks founded on ancient tradition made in the late eighteenth century by Saint-Martin, the 'unknown philosopher', in his often obscure language. Rudolf Steiner spoke about the doctrine of sin,[4] the human sinner and the fact that human beings were originally not intended to descend so deeply into the material world. He said that the form of this doctrine found in the work of Saint-Martin was 'still quite a good version of it'. In his book *Des erreurs et de la vérité*[5] Saint-Martin also discussed the state and society and the nature of politics. He, too, described what human beings would be like if they had remained in their former condition and not experienced the Fall. They would all be rulers and kings, just as they had been before the Fall, ruling not over their fellow men and women but over other beings about which, however, Saint-Martin volunteers no further information. Political society would never have existed for human beings. But as a result of the Fall they lost their 'ancient sceptre' and political society came into being. However, they retained the ability to work and regain their old rights through their efforts. One who is better able to avoid the dark consequences of the Fall or whose efforts raise him above them to a greater extent (whereby a genuine inequality would arise among human beings who had once all been equal), such a one is called to rule over those others. This, said Saint-Martin, is the true origin of rulership by some over others on this earth.[6]

Through all this there resound ancient Mystery truths and also facts created by the ancient Mysteries. The Mystery centres were the places where in olden times people worked at refining and purifying their astral bodies of 'kama' and at overcoming as far as they could the consequences of the Fall. Through doing this they were able to share in the light of the spiritual world and in the inspiring revelations of its beings. Such individuals did indeed seem called to govern their fellows as rulers or kings and by doing so to serve them. We see how people of ancient times looked back to the light of human origins. Out of this grew the principles according to which these cultures were governed.

Let us remember in this connection the conditions and basis of rulership in the far past of Europe.[7] There, under the secret guidance of the 'European brahmins', members of the warrior or princely caste ruled over a population that had sunk especially deeply into the moral darkness of the second Fall, as it has been called, that had overwhelmed a large portion of humanity during the fourth era of Atlantis, the time of the primeval Turanian sub-race.[8] Here, too, individuals, castes or races who had been more successful in repelling the consequences of that Fall ruled over the others, setting them an example. That is why the ideals of the warrior caste, resolute courage and valour, found their way into the European population. Populations who had sunk very low were able to raise themselves upwards over the course of millennia in the manner described earlier.[7]

Thus, in the events brought about by the moral and spiritual decline that set in during the middle period of Atlantis, we discover the origins of the type of rulership that developed later. This is corroborated in other statements made by Rudolf Steiner about Saint-Martin[9] which culminated in an indication pointing to these very events in Atlantis.

Steiner remarked that Saint-Martin was one of the last who was consciously aware of being a pupil of Jakob Böhme, and that his book

131

Des erreurs et de la vérité was entirely founded on Böhme's work. Saint-Martin knew that the right kind of political thoughts about the structure of society must come out of the spiritual world, and such are the thoughts contained in his book. In it 'there is a very definite and important idea, and it is significant to find it being given prominence in Saint-Martin's political thinking. He is writing about "original adultery by human beings". This adultery, he says, took place at a time when there was as yet no sexual relationship between man and woman on earth, so he cannot be meaning adultery in the usual sense of the word. He means something quite different over which, however, he throws an impenetrable veil. It is something about which the Bible also speaks in the passage: "And the sons of the gods saw the daughters of men that they were fair; and they took them wives of all which they chose." This was the event that brought about all the confusion in the world of Atlantis and which is also connected in a mysterious way with the fact that human beings turned their elementary spiritual nature into something sensual.'[10]

Finally we may note that the opposite of what we have seen to be the legitimate principle of rulership in ancient times can also be clearly described. This is the principle of tyranny or despotism in the later sense of these words. It came about when the ruler exercised his power without having undergone a process of purification, when he was still a slave of his own personal urges and passions and therefore misused his power in an egoistic way. As a result he was easily led by more or less dark spiritual powers who possessed him. This phenomenon appeared most clearly at the time of the Roman Caesars.[11]

*

The great healing counterforce working against the Luciferic temptation in human evolution is the redemptive force of the Christ-impulse. Side by side with the Luciferic temptation this force worked and continues to work throughout the many stages and periods of history. It makes it possible for people gradually to overcome the effects of the Fall and weave them, transformed, into the various aspects of their being. Among those who take it into themselves it builds a kingdom that can, in the end, overcome the 'state', making it redundant. This is possible, even now, within an existing state, if this is taken to mean a human and legal arrangement that prescribes and enforces a certain minimum standard of moral behaviour of its citizens amongst each other. Those who anyway bear these standards within themselves remain free of the law, even though outwardly it applies to them as well. Inwardly it does not touch them because with their ego they live in a sphere that lies above it. In their own inner being they experience as a matter of course and in full freedom the same moral intuitions out of which the law of the state, in so far as it is spiritually and humanly justified, has emerged.

Through the power of Christ the human being can transform his astral body, which means that he purifies his passions. To the extent to which he achieves this the spirit-self or Manas arises in him or descends upon him. He becomes more like his angel. Hand in hand with this goes the transformation of brain-bound thinking, capable of grasping only the dead forces of the sense-perceptible world, into the capacity for spiritual imagination that embraces, among other things, the sphere of social life. Out of the community-building work of the Holy Spirit fraternity, brotherly love, arises amongst human beings who have reached this stage. The 'Community of Philadelphia' is formed in which the Christ-impulse can begin to work in social life.

This is intended to take place in a more general way during the sixth post-Atlantean era whose culture is to be founded on the unfolding of the spirit-self, just as that of the fifth era is founded on the unfolding of the consciousness soul. This will be the culmination, the highest point, to be achieved during the seven post-Atlantean eras. It is to unfold especially in the eastern world of the Slavs where today its darkest counter-image is in force.

If the nations of the west can be said to be political by nature and the nations of central Europe non-political, then the Russians could be described as being anti-political. This was formulated by Rudolf Steiner in discussing a potential evolution from the political past to a post-political or supra-political future. Just as the political age was preceded by the pre-political times of the theocracies, so will it be followed by a post-political one. In the pre-political age human beings were connected in the ancient way with the spiritual world, while post-political times will arise with a new spirituality, filled with the Christ-impulse, that will work right down into social life.

Rudolf Steiner described the future cultural era of Manas or the spirit-self as follows: 'It will be a time when human beings will possess a common wisdom to a far higher degree than is the case today . . . This will begin when there is a sense that the most individual part of the human being is at the same time the most general. What is today regarded as individual is not, in actual fact, anything individual in a higher sense. Today the fact that human beings argue and have different opinions is thought to be caused by their having individual personalities . . . But this is because things are seen from a lower standpoint . . . In fact, human beings will be most peaceful and harmonious when they are most individual. While they are not yet overshadowed by the spirit-self they still have differing opinions, but these opinions are not felt to belong to their deepest inner being.

'So far there exist only a few precursors of what can inwardly be felt to be true; these are the truths of mathematics and geometry. There can be no argument about these . . . In the cultural era of Manas the sources of truth will be increasingly sensed within the strong individual personality of each human being, and at the same time there will be agreement about what is felt to be a higher truth, just as is the case now in mathematics. Since these truths are the least important, people can agree about them even today. But other truths are the subject of argument not because there can be two different correct opinions about something but because people are not yet able to recognize and combat all the personal sympathies and antipathies that come between them . . . Those who can look more deeply into the essence of things find it . . . impossible to argue about the higher essence of these things; the only possibility is to develop towards it. When this is achieved, a truth discovered in one soul will be exactly the same truth as that discovered in another; there will then be no more argument. This is what will guarantee real peace and true fraternity, because there is only one truth and this truth really has something to do with the spiritual sun. Think how all the different plants grow correctly; each individual plant grows towards the sun, and there is only one sun. In a similar way, when the spirit-self enters into human beings during the sixth era, there will be a spiritual sun towards which all human beings will strive and in which all will find agreement. This is the grand perspective towards which we can look forward in the sixth era . . . It will be a very important cultural era . . . because through wisdom it will bring peace and fraternity . . . not only for select individuals but for all human beings who come within the normal process of evolution.'[12]

In another context Rudolf Steiner expressed something that can only be understood if it is perceived to be inwardly linked with the perspective for the future just quoted. He said that in the future, out of the force of the increasingly strong Christ-impulse, something would be generated in human souls that would make it impossible for any kind of government to be founded on ambition or vanity, or even on prejudices or errors: 'It is possible to find principles of government that exclude vanity, ambition, prejudices, or even stupidity or error; but this is only possible through a right and concrete comprehension of the Christ-impulse. Such impulses will not be enacted by parliaments. They will come into the world in other ways, for it is the direction in which evolution is flowing. In addition to the longing to comprehend Christ in world evolution, it is the direction of the longing to let Christ live in the social evolution of mankind.'[13]

This will be one stream, the upward one. Beside it will flow another, downwards. A great divide will appear between the two and there will be far-reaching disputes, battles and struggles in the effort to overcome and heal the downward stream by the upward one. These times are approaching and their advent can be felt even today.

NOTES

Abbreviations:

Vol I: Refers to Karl Heyer *Studienmaterialien zur Geschichte des Abendlandes. Band I: Von der Atlantis bis Rom* (From Atlantis to Rome). The present translation of Volume II of the *Studienmaterialien* is made primarily from the 1956 German edition, while taking into account the 1985 edition. The page numbers given for *Vol I* refer to the 1985 German edition.
RS: Rudolf Steiner.
GA: Bibliographical Number in the complete works of Rudolf Steiner in German.

The Germanic Peoples

1　　See table in *Vol I*, p.21. Also RS *At the Gates of Spiritual Science*, Rudolf Steiner Press, London 1986, (GA 95), Lecture of 1 September 1906.

2　　Hans Erhard Lauer *Die Volksseelen Europas*, Stuttgart 1964.

3　　RS *The Mission of the Individual Folk-Souls in Relation to Teutonic Mythology*, Rudolf Steiner Press, London 1970, (GA 121), Lecture of 16 June 1910.

4　　RS *The Gospel of St John*, Anthroposophic Press, New York 1984, (GA 103), Lecture of 22 May 1908.

5　　RS *The Apocalypse of St John*, Rudolf Steiner Press, London 1985, (GA 104), Lecture of 19 June 1908.

6　　My italics. See also *Vol I*, p.171f.

7　　Tacitus *Germania, A treatise on the situation, manners and inhabitants of Germany*, London, no date, Transl. J. Brodie.

8　　RS *The Mission of the Individual Folk-Souls in Relation to Teutonic Mythology*, op. cit., Lecture of 16 June 1910.

9　　RS *The Being of Man and his Future Evolution*, Rudolf Steiner Press, London 1981, (GA 107), Lecture of 3 May 1909.

10　　See *Vol I*, p.23.

11　　RS *Impulses of the Past and Future in Social Occurrences*. Typescript R 87 at Rudolf Steiner Library, London, (in GA 190), Lecture of 12 April 1919.

12　　Karl Heyer *Rechts- und staatsgeschichtliche Entwicklungslinien*, Stuttgart 1922. Also Ludwig Thieben *Strafrecht, Mensch und Schicksal*, Basel 1930. Also Roman Boos *Der Gesamtarbeitsvertrag nach schweizerischem Recht*, Munich & Leipzig 1916, and *Neugeburt des deutschen Rechts. Ein Beitrag zur Überwindung des corpus juris*, Munich & Berlin 1934.

13   Rudolf von Jhering *Der Geist des römischen Rechts*, Part I, 1878, p.179.

14   See, for example, Paul Wilutzky *Vorgeschichte des Rechts*, Berlin 1903, p.67.

15   Ludwig Thieben *Strafrecht, Mensch und Schicksal*, op. cit.

16   Ibid.

17   See *Vol I*, Part II, 'Rome'.

18   RS *The Four Seasons and the Archangels*. Rudolf Steiner Press, London 1968, (GA 229), Lecture of 6 October 1923.

19   RS *The Fall of the Spirits of Darkness*, Rudolf Steiner Press, Sussex 1992, (GA 177), Lecture of 12 October 1917.

20   RS *History of the Middle Ages until the Time of the Great Discoveries*, Typescript R 89 at Rudolf Steiner Library, London, (GA 51), Lecture of 25 October 1904.

21   Hans Erhard Lauer, *Die Volksseelen Europas*, op. cit.

22   Martin Lintzel *Karl der Grosse und Widukind*, Hamburg 1935, p.13.

23   *Vol I*, p.159.

24   RS *Inner Impulses of Human Evolution. The Mexican Mysteries and the Knights Templar*, Anthroposophic Press, New York 1984, (GA 171), Lecture of 7 September 1916.

25   RS *Riddles of Philosophy*, Anthroposophic Press, New York 1973, (GA 18), p.69.

26   RS *Historical Foundation for the Formation of Judgement on the Social Question*, Typescript R 41 at Rudolf Steiner Library, London, (GA 185a), Lecture of 23 November 1918.

27   Rudolf Steiner also pointed out that the abstract monotheism that came in from the south-east through the theocratic-Jewish element could equally not have arisen out of the Germanic element. In his book on the culture and religion of the Germanic peoples Wilhelm Grönbech cited a great deal of evidence for the fact that the monarchic concept of the state was entirely foreign to the freedom-loving nature of these peoples.

28   See also *Vol I*, p.19-21.

29   See *Vol I*, p.11.

30   See Ernst Uehli's essay 'Der Staufer Friedrich II' in the journal *Erziehungskunst*, IX 5/6, December 1935 to February 1936, p.219f.

31   RS *The Mission of the Individual Folk-Souls in Relation to Teutonic Mythology*, op. cit., Lecture of 12 June 1910.

32   See *Vol I*, p.161 and 237.

33   See *RS Aus schicksaltragender Zeit*, Dornach 1959, (GA 64), Lecture
        of 14 January 1915. Also *Destinies of Individuals and of Nations*, Rudolf
        Steiner Press, London 1987, (GA 157), Lecture of 19 January 1915.

The Middle Ages

Section 1.

1   *Vol I*, p.97-99.

2   See *Vol I*, especially p.100-103.

3   See *RS Occult History*, Rudolf Steiner Press, London 1982, (GA 126),
        Lecture of 1 January 1911

4   St Augustine of Hippo (354-430) *De civitate Dei* (The City of God),
        London & Cambridge, Massachusetts 1972, transl. William M. Green,
        Book 22, Chapter 30.

5   See Heyer *Das Wunder von Chartres*, Basel 1938.

6   See *Vol I*, p.100.

7   See Heyer 'Sozialimpulse des Mittelalters und ihre Wandlung zur
        Dreigliederung des sozialen Organismus' in the journal *Das Goetheanum*
        VI 27 of 3 July 1927, p.214.

8   See especially *Vol I*, p.35f.

9   Charles IV, crowned in Rome in 1355, set out to make the Holy Roman
        Empire a specifically German institution. He defined the rights of the
        electors in the Golden Bull of 1356 and the changes he made were reflected
        in the final evolution of the empire's title: *Sacrum Romanum imperium
        nationis Germanicae* (Holy Roman Empire of the German Nation).

Section 2.

1   This description follows Josef Reinkens *Die Geschichtsphilosophie des
        heiligen Augustinus*, Schaffhausen 1866, p.14-33.

2   In the original: *Remota itaque iustitia quid sunt regna nisi magna latrocinia?*
        (*De civitate Dei* 4, chap.4).

3   Comp. Joseph Mausbach *Die Ethik des heiligen Augustinus*, Vol.I, Freiburg
        1909, p.232, 233, 326-350.

4   RS *The Mission of the Individual Folk-Souls in Relation to Teutonic
        Mythology*, op. cit., Lecture of 16 June 1916.

5   In the journal *Die Drei*, V 5 (August 1925), p.337f.

6   RS *History of the Middle Ages until the Time of the Great Discoveries*, op. cit., Lecture of 6 December 1904.

Section 3.

1   See p.14.

2   This view of the 'Holy Roman Empire of the German Nation' does not conflict with another fact, which should also be mentioned: The full title of 'Holy Roman Empire of the German Nation' is relatively late and the addition 'of the German Nation' was originally used officially not to denote the supremacy of the German nation over the Roman Empire but merely to signify the German territories contained within that Empire, namely the Empire not including Italy or Burgundy. This is pointed out by Karl Eder in *Deutsche Geisteswende zwischen Mittelalter und Neuzeit*, Salzburg-Leipzig 1937, p.94. He goes on to show, however, that from the middle of the fifteenth century onwards the title as a whole statement came increasingly to the fore. Our next chapter, 'Medieval Universalism', will show more clearly that in the way people thought and felt in the Middle Ages the Germans were, in fact, accorded a position of dominance in the Holy Roman Empire of the German Nation.

3   See Heyer 'Vom Reiche des Silbernen Königs in der Geschichte' in the journal *Das Goetheanum*, VII 26 of 24 June 1928, p.203f. Also Heyer *Menschheitsfragen der Gegenwart*, Basel 1927, p.62 and 102.

4   Karl Christian Planck *Testament eines Deutschen*, 2nd edition, Jena 1912, p.675.

5   RS *Ideas for a New Europe. Crisis and Opportunity for the West*, Rudolf Steiner Press, Sussex 1992, (GA 196), Lectures of 20, 21 and 22 February 1920; also *Polarities in the Evolution of Mankind*, Rudolf Steiner Press, London 1987, (GA 197), Lecture of 9 March 1920. Also Heyer 'Reichsidee und Gegenwart' in the journal *Die Drei*, IX 3, June 1929, p.185.

6   RS *Ideas for a New Europe*, op. cit, Lecture of 21 February 1920.

7   See Note 5 above, 'Reichsidee und Gegenwart', p.185f, op. cit.

8   See Heyer *Menschheitsfragen der Gegenwart*, op. cit., Chap 5, p.102.

9   RS *The Mission of the Archangel Michael*, Anthroposophic Press, New York 1961, (GA 194), Lecture of 29 November 1919. Also Dante *De monarchia*, II 3.

10   RS *The Karma of Untruthfulness*, Vol.I., Rudolf Steiner Press, London 1988, (GA 173), Lecture of 16 December 1916.

11   See *Vol I*, p.242.

12   RS *Historical Foundation for the Formation of Judgement on the Social Question*, op. cit., Lecture of 15 November 1918.

Section 4.

1   Dante, *De monarchia*, I, 8

2   See a passage in RS *The Karma of Untruthfulness*, Vol I, op. cit., Lecture of 16 December 1916: 'This argument about Charlemagne really has as little point as an argument of three sons about their father. If three sons quarrel amongst each other, the reason is frequently that they are all quite right to call a certain person their father ... Strictly speaking, all three [the western part, the eastern part and the middle - Italy - all emerged from the empire of Charlemagne] are equally justified in tracing themselves back to Charlemagne ...'

3   RS *Der Dornacher Bau als Wahrzeichen geschichtlichen Werdens und künstlerischer Umwandlungsimpulse*, Dornach, (GA 287), Lecture of 18 October 1914 (on the cultural developments of Europe in connection with the Goetheanum building).

4   Hans Spangenberg *Vom Lehnstaat zum Ständestaat*, Munich-Berlin 1912, p.77-78.

5   Leopold von Ranke *Preussische Geschichte*, Vol I, p.108, quoted by Spangenberg, see Note 4 above.

6   Rudolf Steiner was referring to the policies of Philip the Fair (reigned 1285-1314) about whom more will be said later.

7   RS 'The History of Modern Times in the Light of Spiritual Scientific Investigation' in *Anthroposophical News Sheet*, 1934, (GA 73), Lecture of 17 October 1918.

Section 5.

1   RS *A Sound Outlook for Today and a Genuine Hope for the Future*, Typescript C 50 at Rudolf Steiner Library, London, (GA 181), Lecture of 16 July 1918. On this aspect of Henry II (reigned 1002-1024), see also the brief reference in *History of the Middle Ages until the Time of the Great Discoveries*, op. cit., Lecture of 18 October 1904.

2   RS *Discussions with Teachers*, Rudolf Steiner Press, London 1967, (GA 295), Seminar discussion of 28 August 1919. See also *Mysterienwahrheiten und Weihnachtsimpulse. Alte Mythen und ihre Bedeutung*, Dornach 1980, (GA 180), Lecture of 17 January 1918, in which Rudolf Steiner mentioned the fact that the Church, weakened by the wide expansion of its territory and its extensive political activity, endeavoured to regain strength by means of the Crusades. Peter of Amiens and Walter von Habenichts failed to achieve anything. Godfrey of Bouillon worked in a different spirit.

3   RS *A Sound Outlook for Today and a Genuine Hope for the Future*, op. cit., Lecture of 16 July 1918.

4   Georg Wilhelm Friedrich Hegel *Philosophy of History*, 1857, Part 4, Section 2, Chapter 2 'The Crusades'. Rudolf Steiner described the facts in a very similar way.

5   In this connection the Venetian Republic played a special and exceedingly important role for many centuries. Rudolf Steiner made a particular point of linking Venice, in particular, with the reversal of the original spirit of the Crusades. He pointed especially to Enrico Dandolo (1108-1205), saying he was an incarnation of the Ahrimanic spirit. He was the doge of Venice who imposed the Ahrimanic spirit on the true spirit out of which the Crusades had originally sprung. In this connection Steiner mentioned that under this Ahrimanic Venetian influence holy relics became a basis for the creation of capital. As their value rose and fell they were traded like shares on the stock market. RS *A Sound Outlook for Today and a Genuine Hope for the Future*, op. cit., Lecture of 17 July 1918.

6   RS *Discussions with Teachers*, op. cit., Seminar discussion of 28 August 1919. My italics.

Section 6.

1   See the discussion of the old 'imperialisms' on p.20.

2   RS *History of the Middle Ages until the Time of the Great Discoveries*, op. cit., Lecture of 15 November 1904.

3   See *Vol I*, section on 'Rome and Christianity', p.225-237.

4   See p.9.

5   RS *Die Welträtsel und die Anthroposophie*, Dornach 1983, (GA 54), Lecture of 3 December 1905 'Parzifal und Lohengrin'.

6   See *Vol I*, p.12-17 on the leadership structure in Atlantean times.

7   Ernst Uehli 'Der Staufer Friedrich II', op. cit.

8   Contemporary sources tell of Frederick Barbarossa having relics of the Magi brought to Cologne, and he is said to have received gems from ambassadors of Prester John. See Hans Heinrich Frei 'Buddha und Zarathustra im Christus-Impuls' in the journal *Die Drei*, VI 4 [1926], p.257.

9   A remark made by Rudolf Steiner to the author on 2 September 1913.

10   RS *Secrets of the Threshold*, Anthroposophic Press, New York 1987, (GA 147), Lecture of 24 August 1913.

11   See also Alfred Schütze *Dreieinigkeit*, Stuttgart 1935, p.32-33, 57, 70f, 116.

12   RS 'The European Mysteries and their Initiates' in *Anthroposophical Quarterly* 1964, (GA 57), Lecture of 6 May 1909.

13   Ernst Uehli 'Der Staufer Friedrich II', op.cit.

14   See also Heyer 'Sozialimpulse des Mittelalters', op. cit. in the journal *Das Goetheanum* VI 27, 28, 37, 38, especially p.219f.

Section 7.

1   See articles mentioned in previous Note.

2   RS *History of the Middle Ages until the Time of the Great Discoveries,* op. cit., Lecture of 18 October 1904. Similarly in the Lecture of 1 November 1904.

3   Ibid., Lecture of 15 November 1904.

4   RS *The Gospel of St John.* op. cit., Lecture of 30 May 1908.

5   See *Vol I*, p.110 re the Greek *polis.*

6   RS *Die Welträtsel und die Anthroposophie*, op. cit., Lecture of 29 March 1906.

7   See also a much later lecture in RS *Oswald Spengler, Prophet of World Chaos*, Anthroposophic Press, New York 1949, (GA 214), Lecture of 9 August 1922: '... Echoes of the Mysteries may be found throughout Greek and Roman history and even right into the early part of the Middle Ages. I have pointed out that the Lohengrin legend can really only be understood by someone who can trace it back away from the external, physical world to the castle of the Grail belonging to the early or indeed the middle part of the Middle Ages.'

8   RS *The Development of Thought from the 4th to the 19th Century,* Typescript Z 222 at Rudolf Steiner Library, London, (GA 325), Lecture of 16 May 1921.

Section 8.

1   RS *Impulses of the Past and the Future in Social Occurrences*, op. cit., Lecture of 30 March 1919.

2   Ibid.

3   Jakob Burckhardt *The Civilization of the Renaissance in Italy*, London 1960.

4   See *Vol I*, Section on 'Rome', p.118f.

Section 9.

1   F. Keutgen *Der deutsche Staat des Mittelalters*, Jena 1918, p.3.

2   Rudolf Steiner also stated this expressly, for example in *History of the Middle Ages until the Time of the Great Discoveries*, op. cit., Lectures of 15 November and 6 December 1904. See also *Mysterienwahrheiten und Weihnachtsimpulse*, op. cit., Lecture of 17 January 1918.

3   See Georg Steinhausen *Geschichte der deutschen Kultur*, Vol I, Leipzig-Vienna 1913, p.53.

4   Hans Spangenberg *Vom Lehnstaat zum Ständestaat*, op. cit., p.1.

5   RS *History of the Middle Ages until the Time of the Great Discoveries*, op. cit., Lecture of 18 October 1904.

6   See the description given by the well-known nineteenth-century expert on German law, Otto von Gierke in *Das Wesen der menschlichen Verbände*. Also to be mentioned here is Roman Boos *Der Gesamtarbeitsvertrag nach schweizerischem Recht*, op. cit. especially p.144f, in which Boos uses the pointed arch of northern architecture to describe the Germanic capacity for co-operation: Unlike the Romans, individuals gently lean towards one another - while preserving their own inner character - coming together to form something higher that is greater than their sum, namely, the community formed out of inner freedom.

7   RS *History of the Middle Ages until the Time of the Great Discoveries*, op. cit., Lecture of 18 October 1904. This additional freedom and space (despite, in another way, the greater restrictions) in which life was led in the Middle Ages is demonstrated, for example, by the medieval hermits. Their way of life would be totally impossible today in any 'civilized state'. Even in the most liberal community the state itself, together with police, financial authorities and the military would soon put a stop to it!

8   This peaceful existence side by side of the various branches of life with their shared aim of *bonum commune* is quite rightly described by Alois Dempf in *Christliche Staatsphilosophie in Spanien*, Salzburg 1937, p.29, as being intrinsic to the Christian Middle Ages. 'Only at that time was there such a rich and varied pattern among the many corporations. It is difficult for us to imagine this today because a newly-awakened absolutism (beginning in the seventeenth and eighteenth centuries) is once again striving to create an overall unity which dominates the whole of society' (just as was the case earlier on, in Antiquity). Ideas about the state formulated by Francesco de Vittoria (1483-1546), which most certainly belong to this medieval, Christian social impulse, are characterized by Dempf as follows: 'Vittoria takes for granted the corporate laws of the universities which we today are only just beginning to understand anew. In the same way he takes Christianity for granted, the *potestas spiritualis*, as well as the *orbis* or mankind as a whole, and the *potestas saecularis*, the nations and states, the corporations and societies, every kind of social organism, each with its own laws. It is as though for him the only reliable guarantee that can truly protect the legal ordering of society as a totality

is for the whole complex of all the *societates et potestates* to be thoroughly structured in all its manifoldness. Only when all arrangements of law and life are clearly seen and distinguished can all rights be genuinely accorded and secured ... Separate and yet united, the powers of social life stand side by side. They are held together by the goal of *bonum orbis*, the good order and freedom of all social groupings, so that each according to its own laws of life and legality can work with all the others for the perfection of true culture and civilization ...'

9   Georg Wilhelm Friedrich Hegel *Philosophy of History*, 1857, Part 4, Section 2, Chapter 1. Op. cit.

10   See, for example, Hans Spangenberg *Vom Lehnstaat zum Ständestaat*, op. cit.

Section 10.

1   See Heyer 'Arabertum und Islam als weltgeschichtliche Kulturimpuls' in the journal *Die Drei*, II 10/11, p.741-760, especially p.747f, where the effects of Arabism including its tendency towards mechanistic thinking are dealt with in a wider context.

2   See, for example, RS 'How do I find the Christ?' in *Anthroposophical Quarterly* 1970, (GA 182), Lecture of 16 October 1918. Also essays by Hans Friedrich Frei 'Geistesgeschichtliche Entwicklungslinien im Hinblick auf den "Impuls von Gondi-Shapur"' in the journal *Die Drei*, IV 10, 11, 12 (Jan, Feb, March 1925). Consider also the counterpart of the impulse of 666 that was at work in the time of Augustus (*Vol I*, p.205-211).

3   See *Vol I*, Section on 'Rome', p.118f.

4   In the context of the twelve types of thinking and looking at the world relating to the Zodiac, this type is that of 'mathematism'. See also Sigismund von Gleich *Geisteswissenschaft, Kunstoffenbarung und religiöse Lebensanschauung*, manuscript publication 1937, in which von Gleich was concerned particularly with Abraham, whose specific way of thinking was inherited by the Semitic peoples, both Arabs and Jews.

5   R. Kaufmann in Pflugk-Harttung's *Weltgeschichte*, Volume entitled 'Geschichte des Mittelalters', Berlin 1909, p.198.

6   Oswald Spengler *Preussentum und Sozialismus*, Munich 1920, p.47f.

7   Richard Schmidt *Allgemeine Staatslehre*, Leipzig 1903, Vol II, Part II, Chap 1, especially p.464.

8   Jacob Burckhardt *The Civilization of the Renaissance in Italy*, op. cit.

9   See RS *Die Mysterien des Morgenlandes und des Christentums*, Dornach 1960, (GA 144), Lecture of 6 February 1913. During the middle period of the Middle Ages an Arabian Luciferic goddess, with whom Klingsor was united in an unholy alliance, had her seat here. The geological aspect

of this is described by Friedrich Häusler in 'Aus den sizilianischen Rätseln' in the journal *Das Goetheanum* XVI 43. He states that in the vicinity of Calatabellota nature has deposited sulphur and salt on top of one another. The extraction of these two substances is still one of Sicily's chief industries. Medieval alchemists regarded them as representing opposing activities, salt being that of the head and its connection with human thinking, and sulphur that of the metabolism and limbs and their connection with human will. The former activity is in danger of falling under the sway of Ahriman and the latter under that of Lucifer unless the mediating mercurial element, in the human sense, plays its part between the two. The greatest threat to humanity comes when Lucifer and Ahriman form an alliance that excludes the mediating, human element.

This throws light from another angle on that Saracen, Norman state which brought about the alliance between the Saracens, who lived in the dying forces of the head, and the Normans with their wild, wilful nature. Here we have yet another image of that archetypal marriage between the dark magician Klingsor and the Luciferic Iblis, which in the social and political sense resembles the combination of sulphur and salt found in the geology of the region.

10   With regard to this whole paragraph see RS *Die Mysterien des Morgenlandes und des Christentums*, op. cit., Lecture of 6 February 1913. Also the article by Harry Köhler 'Von der Königin Sibilia und dem Herzoge von Terra de Labur' in the journal *Das Goetheanum*, X 22 of 31 May 1931, p.170-173. Also Walter Johannes Stein *The Ninth Century*. *World History in the Light of the Holy Grail*, Temple Lodge Press, London 1991 (see Index for 'Klingsor'). Also Friedrich von Raumer *Geschichte der Hohenstaufen und ihrer Zeit*, Reutlingen 1829, Vol 3, p.45-47.

11   Richard Wagner showed a historical sense for this in his stage directions for *Parsifal*, Act II: Klingsor's castle is to be in a 'rich, Arabian style', and Kundry's dress 'Arabian in style'.

12   Hans Spangenberg *Vom Lehnstaat zum Ständestaat*, op. cit.

13   See the journal *Anthroposophie* VI, 13 November 1924, p.3 (with reference to Helmolt *Weltgeschichte* VI, table between pp.100/101), although the reference to Roger I is wrong here. Roger II (1098-1154) was alive at the relevant time. The year AH 528 is AD 1150. See also S. Hunke *Allahs Sonne über dem Abendland*.

14   See Section 5, Note 5.

15   See Heyer *Geschichtsimpulse des Rosenkreuzertums*, Breslau 1938, p.74.

Section 11.

1   Ibid.

2   See Ernst Uehli *Eine neue Gralsuche*, Stuttgart 1921. Also Walter Johannes Stein *The Ninth Century*, op. cit., which contains valuable material, although it does not actually describe this aspect.

3   See RS *Inner Impulses of Human Evolution. The Mexican Mysteries and the Knights Templar*, op. cit., Lectures of 25 Sep and 2 October 1916. The other statements made by Rudolf Steiner about the tragedy of the Templars are also taken from these lectures.

4   See Carl Julius Weber *Das Ritter-Wesen und die Templer, Johanniter und Marianer*, Vol.2, Stuttgart 1836, p.282f. Also Konrad Schottmüller *Der Untergang des Templer-Ordens*, Vol.I, Berlin 1887, p.54f.

5   RS *Towards Social Renewal*, London 1977.

6   See RS *Kunstgeschichte als Abbild innerer geistiger Impulse*, Dornach 1981, (GA 292), Lecture of 22 October 1917.

7   See *Vol.I*, for example p.12, 40, 75-77.

8   Walter Johannes Stein *Gold in History and in Modern Times*, St George Publications, Spring Valley 1986.

9   See Peter Richard Rohden *Männer, die Geschichte machten*, Vienna 1931, Vol.II, p.129.

10 Leopold von Ranke *Französische Geschichte*, Leipzig 1876, Vol.I, p.34.

11 Regarding the following, see Richard Scholz *Die Publizistik zur Zeit Philipps des Schönen und Bonifaz' VIII*, Stuttgart 1903, p.375f, and Walther Schücking *Die Organisation der Welt*, Leipzig 1909, p.28f.

12 See the following historians:
    1. Hans Prutz *Die geistlichen Ritterorden*, Berlin 1908, p.475f.
    2. Engelbert Huber *Die Freimaurerei*, Stuttgart 1934, p.19.
    3. Walther Kienast in Peter Richard Rohden *Männer, die Geschichte machten*, op. cit., p.129f.
    4. Leopold von Ranke *Französische Geschichte*, op. cit.
    5. *Handbuch der Staatengeschichte. Ausland*, ed. Richard Scholz, Berlin 1922, p.26f.

13 See *Vol I*, p.216-218, 222-224.

14 See RS *Inner Impulses of Human Evolution. The Mexican Mysteries and the Knights Templar*, op. cit., Lectures of 25 Sep and 2 October 1916.

15 See Konrad Schottmüller *Der Untergang des Templer-Ordens*, op. cit., Vol.I, p.82.

16 Such a thing is particularly abhorrent to the way a modern state sees itself. It cannot tolerate anything that purports to be its equal; it wants to be above everything. The only thing it can, or must, regard as its equal is another sovereign state with which it merely has to cultivate a relationship in international law or with which it can enter into treaties such as the League of Nations.

17   See RS *Inner Impulses of Human Evolution. The Mexican Mysteries and the Knights Templar*, op. cit., Lecture of 2 October 1916.

18   For example in *Gold in History and in Modern Times*, op. cit. and also in his preface to Friedrich Zacharias Werner *Die Söhne des Tals*, Stuttgart 1927, p.6f.

19   RS *Inner Impulses of Human Evolution. The Mexican Mysteries and the Knights Templar*, op. cit., Lecture of 2 October 1916. Also, with reference to the whole subject, Heyer *Aus dem Jahrhundert der französischen Revolution*, Breslau 1937, especially Chapter II 'Spirituelle Ursprünge und spätere Schicksale sozialer Ideale'. Also Heyer *Die Französische Revolution und Napoleon*, published in manuscript, Kressbronn 1953.

20   See also Heyer *Menschheitsfragen der Gegenwart*, op. cit., Chapter IV 'Sozialimpulse des deutschen Geistes in Vergangenheit und Gegenwart', and Heyer *Geschichtsimpulse des Rosenkreuzertums*, op. cit, p.97, and Heyer *Sozialimpulse des deutschen Geistes im Goethe-Zeitalter*, published in manuscript, Kressbronn 1954.

21   See Karl Falkenstein *Geschichte der drei wichtigsten Ritterorden des Mittelalters*, Dresden 1830, Part I, p.94.

22   Jules Michelet *Geschichte der Französischen Revolution*, Vol.3/4, Chapter 29. My italics.

23   The French have a genius for managing events in this way. Consider, for example, the arrangements made for the signing of the Versailles peace treaty in 1919 to make this a counterpart of the proclamation of the German Kaiser that had taken place in the same Hall of Mirrors at Versailles on 18 January 1871. Regarding the psychology of the French people, in which such things are inherent, see Heyer 'Das französische Wesen und die gegenwärtige Weltlage' in *Korrespondenz der Anthroposophischen Arbeitsgemeinschaft*, II 10 (1933).

24   Support for the idea of conscious revenge being taken against the French royal house (and the church) for what had been done to the Templars could also be read into the allegedly threatening letter sent to the brother of Louis XVI, the text of which is included in Heyer *Aus dem Jahrhundert der französischen Revolution*, Breslau 1937, p.98. However, it is not clear whether this letter was genuine, but it is significant that such ideas should have been part of the atmosphere of the time.

25   As did Walter Johannes Stein in *Gold in History and in Modern Times*, op. cit.

Section 12.

1   RS *Mysterienwahrheiten und Weihnachtsimpulse*, op. cit., Lecture of 17 January 1918.

2   See previous section.

3   Erich Maschke *Der deutsche Ordensstaat*, Hamburg 1935, p.16.

4   Roxane Troeltsch *Schlüssel im Meer. Gibraltar, Malta, Zypern, Suez*, Munich 1936, p.49-61, contains a more novelistic approach to the character of Hompesch. In *Der Kampf gegen den Geist und das Testament Peters des Grossen*, Stuttgart 1922, Ludwig Polzer-Hoditz also referred briefly to this subject when he said that Hompesch only gave up Malta 'because he had no other possibility but to choose between Russia' (who wanted Malta as well as Constantinople as marine bases) 'and France and was forced, perhaps, to choose France.'

5   Carl Julius Weber *Das Ritterwesen und die Templer, Johanniter und Marianer*, op. cit., Vol.2, p.374f.

6   Paul I's efforts with regard to the Hospitallers may also be linked to efforts being made to 'bring certain secret brotherhoods from the west to Russia', about which Rudolf Steiner spoke, also making the connection with Paul I and even Catherine the Great. See RS *Things of the Present and of the Past in the Spirit of Man*, (GA 167), Typescript C 42 at Rudolf Steiner Library, London, Lecture of 4 April 1916.

7   See Heyer, eight articles 'Der Deutschritterorden und die Ursprünge des späteren Preussens' in the journal *Die Drei* VIII 2, 3, 4 (May, June, July 1928).

8   See Erich Maschke *Der deutsche Ordensstaat*, op. cit., p.31.

9   See articles mentioned in Note 7 above.

10   RS *Die geistigen Hintergründe des ersten Weltkrieges*, Dornach 1974, (GA 174b), Lecture of 12 March 1916.

11   RS *Between Death and Rebirth*, Rudolf Steiner Press, London 1975, (GA 141), Lecture of 22 December 1912.

12   On the Hospitallers and the Templars see also the essay by Emil Bock 'Zur Ketzergeschichte' in the journal *Die Christengemeinschaft* XXV 2 (February 1953), p.53.

Section 13.

1   This aspect is beautifully described in Ernst von Hippel *Die Krieger Gottes. Die Regel Benedikts als Ausdruck frühchristlicher Gemeinschaftsbildung*, Halle 1936.

Section 14.

1   See p.20, and also RS *Foundations of Esotericism*, Rudolf Steiner Press,

London 1982, (GA 93a), Lecture of 8 October 1905: 'The structure of the church goes back to the same Dionysius who elaborated the teachings about the heavenly hierarchies. The external church was to be nothing more than an image of the inner hierarchy of the heavens.'

2   RS *Three Lectures on Roman Catholicism*, Typescript Z 65 at Rudolf Steiner Library, London, (GA 198), Lecture of 3 June 1920.

3   RS *The Philosophy of Freedom*, Rudolf Steiner Press, London 1979 (GA 4).

4   Emile Mâle *L'art religieux de XIIIe siècle en France*, Paris 1899, p.441.

5   At an earlier stage a similar transition seems to have taken place around the time of the Mystery of Golgotha, according to the following sentences by Rudolf Steiner in *Reincarnation and Karma. Their Significance in Modern Culture*, Anthroposophic Press, New York 1985, (GA 135), Lecture of 21 February 1912: 'In ancient times before the Mystery of Golgotha there was still an old form of clairvoyance, as well as magical will forces. This lasted even into the early Christian centuries. But everything of the ancient clairvoyance that still came into the world from higher realms during these late centuries was only evil and demonic. The Gospels everywhere describe demonic beings surrounding Christ Jesus.'

6   Karl Eder *Deutsche Geisteswende zwischen Mittelalter und Neuzeit*, op. cit., p.38.

Section 15.

1   This figure (more exactly 354 years and 4 months) is given by Johannes Trithemius (d. 1516 in Würzburg) in his work *De septem secundeis, id est, intelligentiis, sive Spiritibus Orbes post Deum moventibus, reconditissimae scientiae et eruditionis Libellus*. An important aspect of Rudolf Steiner's teaching also points to seven successive archangelic or planetary periods.

2   See Vol.I, p.21f.

3   Page 182 of the journal *Anthroposophie* IX 42 (10 October 1927) shows a notebook entry by Rudolf Steiner dated 1924. Here the dates for the Gabriel era (working backwards) are given as 1879-1510. The note further shows - evidently very approximate - dates for the preceding archangelic eras which, according to this, were of varying duration.

4   Walter Johannes Stein's article 'Weltgeschichte vom Seelischen aus gesehen' in the journal *Das Goetheanum* IV 40, 4 October 1925, p.315f.

5   See RS *Anthroposophical Leading Thoughts*, Rudolf Steiner Press, London 1973, (GA 26), 'At the Gates of the Spiritual Soul [Consciousness Soul]. How Michael in the spiritual world is preparing for his Earth Mission through the conquest of Lucifer.' 30 November, 7 & 14 December 1924.

6   RS *Occult History*, Rudolf Steiner Press, London 1982, (GA 126), Lecture of 28 December 1910.

7   RS *Anthroposophical Leading Thoughts*, op. cit. 7 December 1924, and RS *Occult History*, op. cit., Lecture of 28 December 1910.

8   Hans Spangenberg *Vom Lehnstaat zum Ständestaat*, op. cit., p.93.

9   See *Rechts- und staatsgeschichtliche Entwicklungslinien*, op. cit. See also Heyer 'Die Entwicklung des Rechts in Ost, Mitte und West' in *Das Goetheanum* II 23, 24, 25 (January 1923), particularly p.189.

10   RS *Anthroposophical Leading Thoughts*, op. cit. 14 December 1924.

11   RS *Eleven European Mystics*, Rudolf Steiner Publications, New York 1971, (GA 7).

12   RS *Anthroposophical Leading Thoughts*, op. cit., 14 December 1924.

13   RS *Eleven European Mystics*, op. cit. Preface to the German Edition of 1923. My italics.

14   See Heyer *Geschichtsimpulse des Rosenkreuzertums*, op. cit.

15   On this work see Heyer 'Der Friede und die Harmonie der Religionen' in the journal *Das Goetheanum* XI 18 (1932), p.145f.

16   In a lecture given on 10 April 1921 at the Goetheanum in Dornach I endeavoured to describe the nature of these social impulses more closely, especially as expressed in Cusa's *De concordantia catholica* (1433). See the journal *Die Drei* I 5/6 (1921), p.571-586.

17   This is also acknowledged and stressed by, for example, Gerhard Kallen in his book *Nikolaus von Cues als politischer Erzieher*, Leipzig 1937, p.18/19f.

18   Cusa *De concordantia catholica*, III 11.

19   RS *The Origins of Natural Science*, Anthroposophic Press, New York 1985, (GA 326), Lecture of 24 December 1922.

20   See Heyer *Geschichtsimpulse des Rosenkreuzertums*, op. cit.

21   See RS *Anthroposophical Leading Thoughts*, op. cit. 14 December 1924.

22   See RS *Between Death and Rebirth*, op. cit., (GA 141), Lecture of 22 December 1912.

23   See Heyer *Geschichtsimpulse des Rosenkreuzertums*, op. cit., p.54f.

24   See Vol I, p.239f.

25   See Ernst von Hippel *Mensch und Gemeinschaft*, Leipzig 1935, p.90f.

26   See Heyer *Rechts- und staatsgeschichtliche Entwicklungslinien*, op. cit., p.11f.

27   See RS *Old and New Methods of Initiation*, Rudolf Steiner Press, London 1991, (GA 210), Lecture of 24 February 1922.

28   See Note 27 above. Also the article by Ulrich Blasberg in the journal *Anthroposophie*, VII 29 (19 July 1925, p.122).

29   See, for example, B. F. Keutgen *Der deutsche Staat im Mittelalter*, Jena 1918, p.178f.

30   See Note 29 above, p.181.

31   R. Sternfeld *Französische Geschichte*, Leipzig 1911, p.69f.

32   The House of Valois reigned 1328-1498.

33   J. Calmette in Peter Richard Rohden *Männer, die Geschichte machten*, op. cit. Vol II, p.196f.

34   See Heyer *Der Machiavellismus*, Berlin 1918, Appendix: 'Der Fürst als machiavellistischer Politiker'. Also Heyer *Machiavelli und Ludwig XIV*, published in manuscript, Kressbronn 1951.

The Mongolian Peoples

1   Regarding this similarity in their nature, see RS *Unsere atlantischen Vorfahren*, Berlin 1909, p.40. Sigismund von Gleich, in his book *Der Mensch der Eiszeit und Atlantis*, Stuttgart 1936, shows the strong possibility that the Mongolians are also the physical descendants of the primeval Turanians. See especially the chapter 'Der zweite Sündenfall unter den Urturaniern', p.69-79, and also p.89 and 126ff.

2   Regarding this betrayal, see RS *Occult Science*, Rudolf Steiner Press, London 1979, (GA 13).

3   Sigismund von Gleich 'Turanisch-mongolische Wesenszüge' in *Korrespondenz der Anthroposophischen Arbeitsgemeinschaften*, IV 6, March 1935, p.5-12. Both this article and the book mentioned in Note 1 above contain much valuable information on this subject.

4   RS *The Gospel of St Matthew*, Rudolf Steiner Press, London 1965, (GA 123), Lecture of 1 September 1910.

5   ibid.

6   ibid.

7   ibid.

8   See Joachim Barckhausen *Das gelbe Weltreich*, Berlin 1935, p.63.

9 The she-wolf also appears as a significant symbol in connection with the origins of Rome and I have endeavoured to characterize this 'wolf' aspect of Roman history (see *Vol.I*, p.121, 219f). However, there is insufficient justification for drawing too close a comparison between the Romans and the Turanians. Despite everything, the Romans do belong to the advancing stream of human evolution and they are connected with the western development of the human individuality. It is also true, however, that especially in their later, decadent, period they were infected by a different soul element as well. The world of the Romans had two faces, like Janus. It was able to develop in a positive direction, but it could also fall prey to powers of decline. Valentin Tomberg (see *Vol.I*) described the Roman world as a 'stream of compromise' between Iran and Turan which therefore cannot last forever; individuals would have to decide for the one or the other.
There is also another way of looking at the 'wolf' aspect of the Turanians and the she-wolf of Rome. Like the wolf Fenrir, the Turanian wolf lives in old, atavistic clairvoyance and represents a relationship with the spiritual world that is dark and magical. The Roman she-wolf, on the other hand, represents that 'battle against the spirit' through which the human being first becomes a personality, an ego, that could, if spirituality is darkened, become exclusively interested in the physical world. From this situation, however, it is possible for the ego to find a direct path to the new, Christian spirituality, whereas no such direct path leads from the misuse of atavistic spirituality.

10 See Emil Bock *Cäsaren und Apostel*, Stuttgart 1937, p.95.

11 RS *History of the Middle Ages until the Time of the Great Inventions and Discoveries*, op. cit., Lecture of 1 November 1904.

12 RS *At the Gates of Spiritual Science*, op. cit., Lecture of 28 August 1906.

13 RS *The Spiritual Foundation of Morality. Francis of Assisi and the Mission of Love*, Anthroposophical Publishing Company, London 1955, (GA 155), Lecture of 29 May 1912.

14 See also *Vol.I*, p.23f.

15 RS *The History of the Middle Ages until the Time of the Great Inventions and Discoveries*, op. cit., Lecture of 1 November 1904. Also RS *Der Ring der Nibelungen*, Lecture of 5 May 1905. See also Ernst Uehli 'Der Staufer Friedrich II' op. cit., p.221.

16 RS *Foundations of Esotericism*, op. cit., Lecture of 5 November 1905.

17 Dr Maria Von Nagy 'Attila (Ein Kapitel zur Mission des Bösen)', in the journal *Das Goetheanum*, XV 3, p.20-23.

18 See p.74 regarding the sequence of these archangel or planetary ages.

19 See Note 13 above.

20 A selection of the literature is as follows: Harold Lamb *Dschingis-Khan,*

Beherrscher der Erde, Leipzig 1928; Michael Prawdin 1. *Tschingis-Chan. Der Sturm aus Asien*, Stuttgart-Berlin 1934, and 2. *Das Erbe Tschingis-Chans*, Stuttgart-Berlin 1935; Joachim Barckhausen *Das gelbe Weltreich. Lebensgeschichte einer Macht*, Berlin 1935. A historical novel by Emanuel Stickelberger *Der Reiter auf dem fahlen Pferd. Ein Buch vom Mongolen Dschinggis-Khan und seinem abendländischen Gegenspieler*, Stuttgart 1937, may also be mentioned here.

21   See also Heyer *Wesen und Wollen des Nationalsozialismus*, Basel 1991, Chapter 8, in which 'internal mongolization' is discussed in an endeavour to reach some understanding of why National Socialism came about.

22   RS *Inner Impulses of Human Evolution. The Mexican Mysteries and the Knights Templar*, op. cit., Lecture of 17 September 1916.

23   Ibid, Lecture of 24 September 1916.

24   See Hans Erhard Lauer in the journal *Wie pflegt man Anthroposophie heute in zeitgemässer Art?*, Basel 1953, p.35, 36.

25   Also the poem 'Die Tartarenschlacht bei Wahlstatt' by Gustav Pfizer in *Dichtungen episch-lyrischer Gattung*, Stuttgart & Tübingen 1840, p.233-338.

26   RS *Inner Impulses of Human Evolution. The Mexican Mysteries and the Knights Templar*, op. cit.

27   Ibid, Lectures of 25 September and 2 October 1916.

28   See, for example, 'Attila' by A. Alföldi (Budapest) in Peter Richard Rohden *Männer, die Geschichte machten*, op. cit., Vol.I, p.231.

29   For this and all further descriptions of Genghis Khan and the Mongols see the literature in Note 20 above, and also the essay 'Dschingis-Khan' by G. Vernadskij in Peter Richard Rohden *Männer, die Geschichte machten*, op. cit., p.90f.

30   See Vernadskij, Note 29 above.

31   The designation 'Mongols of the blue of heaven' expressly links the Mongolians with the majesty of the 'Ever-blue sky' or the 'Great Spirit' whose tool Genghis Khan saw himself to be. The attribute 'sky-blue' also contains other connotations when applied to the Mongolians. It expresses the attitude of soul of these tribes by implying that they bore within them a mood generated by the blue of the heavens, a feeling of reverence towards the infinite spaces of the universe which gather up the human being in the ancient Atlantean sense, making him lose his individuality and putting impulses for action into his passive soul.

32   Translator's note: For a description of this see Maurice Collis *Marco Polo*, London 1959.

33   See *Vol.I*, p.66-71.

34   RS *The Mission of the Individual Folk-Souls in Relation to Teutonic Mythology*, op. cit., Lecture of 12 June 1910 (morning).

35   RS *Universe, Earth and Man*, Rudolf Steiner Press, London 1987, (GA105), Lecture of 10 August 1908.

36   RS *Inner Impulses of Human Evolution. The Mexican Mysteries and the Knights Templar*, op. cit., Lecture of 24 September 1916.

37   See Note 20, p.240f.

38   See RS *The Karma of Vocation*, Anthroposophic Press, New York 1984, (GA 172), Lecture of 19 November 1916, where Rudolf Steiner mentioned *Der Geist des chinesischen Volkes*, Jena 1917, by Ku Hung-Ming. See also Heyer *Menschheitsfragen der Gegenwart*, Basel 1927, Chapter 'Das Ost-West-Problem und seine Lösung' p.57f.

39   RS *Egyptian Myths and Mysteries*, Anthroposophic Press, New York 1987, (GA 106), Lecture of 12 September 1908. See also *Universe, Earth and Man*, op. cit., Lecture of 14 August 1908. Also *From Jesus to Christ*, Rudolf Steiner Press, London 1973, (GA 131), Lecture of 12 October 1911.

40   For example RS *The Spiritual Beings in the Heavenly Bodies and in the Kingdoms of Nature*, Rudolf Steiner Publishing Company, London 1951, (GA 136), Lecture of 13 April 1912.

41   See RS *Between Death and Rebirth*, op. cit., Lecture of 22 December 1912. Also Heyer *Geschichtsimpulse des Rosenkreuzertums*, op. cit., p.20f.

42   See Barckhausen *Das gelbe Weltreich*, op. cit., p.176; also p.151, 163; and for what follows see also p.182.

43   Michael Prawdin *Das Erbe Tschingis-Chans*, op. cit., p.265f.

44   RS *Inner Impulses of Human Evolution. The Mexican Mysteries and the Knights Templar*, op. cit, Lecture of 24 September 1916.

45   This doubtless refers to Marco Polo's short description of Japan luxuriating in gold. He never saw that country and mistakenly located it very far to the east of the Chinese mainland. The description was one of the documents on which Columbus based his plan to sail westwards from Europe in search of this Dorado. (See O. Nachod 'Japan' in Pflugk-Harttung's *Weltgeschichte*, Volume 'Geschichte des Orients', Berlin 1910, p.615.)

46   RS *Historical Foundation for the Formation of Judgement on the Social Question*, op. cit., Lecture of 23 November 1918.

47   Ibid.

48   Ibid.

49   Michael Prawdin *Das Erbe Tschingis-Chans*, op. cit., p.270-275.

50   Sigismund von Gleich 'Turanisch-mongolische Wesenszüge', op. cit., p.10.

51   See also the important article by Valentin Tomberg 'Mongolentum in Osteuropa' in the journal *Anthroposophie*, XIII 8 (1931), p.57f. In the context of Russian history as a whole, Tomberg here points to the nature of Mongolian collectivism and its re-emergence in Bolshevism and its organized hatred on the part of the masses for the human individuality.

52   RS *Historical Foundation for the Formation of Judgement on the Social Question*, op.cit., Lecture of 24 November 1918.

53   Wilhelm von Humboldt *The Sphere and Duties of Government*, London 1854. The German title of this work *Ideen zu einem Versuch, die Grenzen der Wirksamkeit des Staates zu bestimmen*, translates literally as 'Ideas towards an attempt to determine the limitations of state power'.

54   RS *From Symptom to Reality in Modern History*, Rudolf Steiner Press, London 1976, (GA 185), Lecture of 18 October 1918.

55   See Note 38 above.

56   For instance very strongly in Emanuel Stickelberger (see Note 20 above).

57   See Note 20 above.

58   Hans Hasso von Veltheim-Ostrau *Berichte meiner zweiten Indienreise 1937/39*, p. 365. A privately-distributed account.

59   Anton Zischka *Japan in der Welt. Die japanische Expansion seit 1854*, Leipzig 1936, p.11.

Appendix 1.

1   RS *Nationalökonomisches Seminar*, Dornach 1973, (GA 341), 3rd discussion, 2 August 1922. We shall return to the later part of this discussion.

2   See *Vol.I*, p.106, 96.

3   See *Vol.I*, Section 1.

4   See *Vol.I*, p.22.

5   Given in 1904 and 1905, of which only inadequate notes remain.

6   See, for example, RS Lecture of 9 November 1904 in *Beiträge zur Rudolf-Steiner-Gesamtausgabe*, Nr 78, p.25f; also RS *Foundations of Esotericism*, op. cit, Lectures of 1 and 28 October 1905.

7   'Those who were world leaders in former times were free of "kama" (free of desires). They had to lay aside all "kama". So long as there were priests in the ancient sense there was no "kama". "Kama" sunders, so people tend to turn against one another. In those days they were not yet able to juxtapose good and evil. Strife and war was something like it is amongst animals today. An intellectual understanding of good and evil only began when manas joined "kama". Then people became aware of why they were fighting one another ... Only when "kama" and manas join together can we talk of conscious strife amongst human beings.' (From inadequate notes taken during a lecture given by Rudolf Steiner on 28 October 1904.)

8   RS in Berlin in *Gäa-Sophia* III, Stuttgart 1929, p.23, also based on inadequate notes.

9   RS Lecture of 3 November 1904 in *Beiträge zur Rudolf-Steiner-Gesamtausgabe*, Nr 71.

10   See *Vol.I*, p.78f.

11   Plato *Politicus*, Book 5.

12   See, for example, the following sentences on 'Plato the Politician': '... The author shows that Plato's philosophical efforts were aimed at a human being who was *neither unpolitical nor, in the modern sense, political*, but for whom there existed as yet *no distinction between politics and non-politics...* ' (From a book review in the literature section of the *Frankfurter Zeitung* of 3 January 1937. My italics.)

13   RS *The Bhagavad Gita and the Epistles of Paul*, Anthroposophic Press, New York 1971, (GA 142), Lectures of 30 and 31 December 1912.

14   The methods by which such qualities were trained included certain games, such as chess, 'the royal game', in which intelligence, ingenuity and calculation are employed with the aim of winning while causing one's

opponent to lose. All such games belong purely in the sphere of 'politics' with its martial, 'Mars' quality that is rationalized in them in the highest degree.

15   See RS *Theosophy*, Rudolf Steiner Press, London 1970, (GA 9).

16   RS *Nationalökonomisches Seminar*, op. cit., 3rd discussion, 2 August 1922.

Appendix 2.

1   This expression and the idea it encompasses has been taken up by many other thinkers; for example Thomas Aquinas (*'Homo est animal sociale, animal civile, animal politicum'*); or Nicholas of Cusa (*'Videmus enim hominem animal esse politicum et civilem et naturaliter ad civilitatem inclinari'*).

2   RS *Inner Impulses of Human Evolution. The Mexican Mysteries and the Knights Templar*, op. cit., Lecture of 16 September 1916.

3   RS *World Economy*, Rudolf Steiner Press, London 1977, (GA 340), Lectures of 24 and 25 July 1922.

4   RS *Philosophy of Freedom*, op. cit.

5   RS *Historical Foundation for the Formation of Judgement on the Social Question*, op. cit., Lecture of 17 November 1918.

Appendix 3.

1   See *Vol 1*, p.240.

2   RS *Inner Impulses of Human Evolution. The Mexican Mysteries and the Knights Templar*, op. cit., Lecture of 17 September 1916.

3   See Heyer *Der Machiavellismus*, op. cit.

4   RS *Social Issues, Meditative Thinking and the Threefold Social Order*, Anthroposophic Press, New York 1991, (GA 334), Lecture of 18 March 1920.

5   RS *Geographic Medicine. The Mystery of the Double*, Mercury Press, Spring Valley 1986, (GA 178), Lecture of 16 November 1917.

6   RS *The Three Paths of the Soul to Christ*, Anthroposophic Press, New York 1942, (GA 143), Lecture of 17 April 1912, in which the Holy Grail and the true Rosicrucian community are discussed.

Appendix 4.

1   See Peter Tischleder *Ursprung und Träger der Staatsgewalt nach der Lehre des hl. Thomas und seiner Schule*, Mönchen-Gladbach 1923, p.14, 26, 38, 40.

2   RS *The Occult Movement in the Nineteenth Century*, Rudolf Steiner Press, London 1973, (GA 254), Lecture of 25 October 1915.

3   Quoted after Albert Steffen in the journal *Das Goetheanum*, IV 29 (1925), p.226.

4   RS *Karmic Relationships*, Vol 3, Rudolf Steiner Press, London 1977, (GA 237), Lecture of 1 August 1924.

5   Louis Claude de Saint-Martin *Des erreurs et de la vérité, ou Les hommes rappelés au principe universel de la science*, Paris 1775.

6   Ibid, II 17.

7   See *Vol.I*, p.23.

8   See Chapter 'The Mongolian Peoples'.

9   See RS *The Fall of the Spirits of Darkness*, Rudolf Steiner Press, Sussex 1992, (GA 177), Lecture of 8 October 1917. Also *Mysterienwahrheiten und Weihnachtsimpulse*, op. cit., Lecture of 25 December 1917.

10   In lectures given on 20 August and 11 September 1916 (Typescripts Z 242 and R 3 at Rudolf Steiner Library, London) contained in GA 272, Rudolf Steiner spoke in more detail about this event in connection with Genesis 6, 2: 'And the sons of the gods saw the daughters of men that they were fair; and they took them wives of all which they chose.' The event in Atlantis is there shown to be a seduction by Ahriman, in comparison with the Fall in Lemurian times, which was a seduction by Lucifer. The consequence of that Ahrimanic impulse is that human beings developed a relationship with the material world that would otherwise not have arisen. Heavenly love became earthly. The human intellect became joined to the physical world in an earthly way, creating materialistic science and founding mechanistic cultures, etc. See also *The True Nature of the Second Coming*, Anthroposophical Publishing Company, London 1961, (GA 118), Lecture of 25 January 1910.

11   See *Vol.I*, Chapter 'Das Cäsarentum', p.190.

12   RS *The Gospel of St John*, op. cit., Lecture of 30 May 1908.

13   RS *Building Stones for an Understanding of the Mystery of Golgotha*, Rudolf Steiner Press, London 1972, (GA 175), Lecture of 12 April 1917.